CHRISTIAN
RESISTANCE

Learning to Defy the World and Follow Christ

D1528221

JAMES SPENCER, PhD

Printed Worldwide
First Printing 2023
First Edition 2023

ISBN: 9798370987854

CHRISTIAN
RESISTANCE

To all those who proclaim, "Jesus is Lord."
"In your struggle against sin you have not yet resisted to the point
of shedding your blood."

Hebrews 12:4

Table of Contents

1 Introduction

Resistance is a form of opposition. We act against some force. It is an action intended to keep at bay the pressures that seek to form us into something we do not wish to become. As Christians, we seek to resist a variety of temptations. We resist the devil (Jam 4:7; 1 Pet 5:9) and sin (Heb 12:4). While we are certainly right to think of sin as rebellion against God that results in immoral acts of various sorts (Rom 13:13; Eph 5:3; Col 3:5), we must also recall that sin is a deviation from God's order. It involves living according to patterns that distort or deny who God is. Sin does not always appear in our overt acts of disobedience but in our passive neglect of God's leading and direction.

For instance, in his discussion of the sin of despair, theologian Jürgen Moltmann notes:

> "To be sure, it is usually said that sin in its original form is man's wanting to be as God. But that is only the one side of sin. The other side of such pride is hopelessness, resignation, inertia and melancholy... Temptation then consists not so much in the titanic desire to be as God, but in weakness, timidity, weariness, not wanting to be what God requires of us."[1]

Here, sin comes in the form of refusal. We refuse to be what God desires us to be and, in the process, deny others the benefits of our being so. Our resistance is directed against God as we stubbornly hold on to our own misdirected desires instead of trusting that any losses we may suffer as we follow God's way will be light and momentary (2 Cor 4:17). When we are willing to, as Moltmann puts it, "be what God requires of us," we resist the world and open ourselves up to the opportunities only God can provide.

I am convinced that one of the biggest challenges we face as Christians is also one of the most mundane: distraction. When Jesus comes to dinner, Martha is distracted by the work of serving (Matt 10:40), whereas Mary sits at the feet of Jesus (10:39). As Martha allows the anxieties of the moment to overwhelm her, she surrenders herself to the conventions of the day and the seemingly necessary obligations that come along with them. Even the conventions and obligations associated with good and right activities, like showing hospitality, can become barriers to sitting at the feet of Jesus. The distraction involves a narrow vision, so Jesus is made secondary to the tasks at hand. Jesus is not the focus of Martha's efforts, but the demands of service and hospitality. Her distraction keeps Martha from choosing "the good portion," as her sister Mary had done (10:42).

To avoid the distraction of Martha, we must learn to resist the urgencies and emergencies that pressure us to dismiss God in favor of the arbitrary expectations we adopt as we live in a broken world. We resist by following God's instruction and attributing all we are and have to Him. We refuse to be lulled into a false sense of self-sufficiency so that we can say in our hearts, "My power and the might of my hand have gotten me this wealth" (Deut 8:17). When we are distracted to the extent that God begins to fade from sight, we will start to see the blessings of God as the fruits of our labor. Beyond the problem of pride, losing the sense that all we have comes from God drains life of theological meaning and pushes us toward frenzied activity because "the reaction to life that has become bare and radically fleeting occurs as hyperactivity, hysterical work, and production."[2]

We begin to believe that the conventions and systems we've established to make the broken world more bearable and manageable deserve our loyalty, devotion, and trust *more than God*. We opt to serve what has been made by human hands rather than serving the Creator (Deut 4:28; Ps 135:15; Rom 6:16). As such, Christian resistance takes the form of obedience to God because by giving our service entirely to Him, we free ourselves from the false gods that set upon us expectations that become de facto idols that "separate us from God, for they effectively act as a screen between God and us."[3] Resisting through obedience brings the clarity necessary to think well about the world. It allows us to identify the human constructions that hinder our discipleship because, through resistance, we live in a manner that acknowledges God's active presence in and among us.

To resist will certainly require us to know the scriptures well, but, in the spirit of James, it is not simply a matter of knowing, but of doing the word of God (Jam 1:19-27; 2:14-26). Resistance requires courage of a sort. It is a courage to trust in the midst of ambiguity and ambivalence. It is a courage to be who God requires us to be even when doing so leads to suffering (Phil 1:27-30; 1 Pet 4:12-17). We will need to resist by what we do and by what we refuse to do. That basic refusal has less to do with a list of "do's and don'ts" than with a commitment to live along the pattern of Christ who obeyed the Father's will even "to the point of death" (Phil 2:8). We need the courage to deny our own desires and agendas, to become "quick to hear, slow to speak, slow to anger," and to be calm in the face of a world in chaos.

This book is intended to explore and offer encouragement through the examination of a variety of concepts. While understanding these concepts intellectually is certainly important, intellectual understanding is not the ultimate goal. Discipleship requires more than intellectual assent. It requires knowledge that comes from experience. It involves knowing God is with us because He has been with us before. We have not simply read of His grace, power, mercy, wisdom, patience, and peace. We have experienced them.

Each of the following chapters is focused on a single concept. The goal is to provide brief treatments of the concept with Bible readings, reflection questions, and prayers that will allow you to consider more deeply how you might test God, in the Malachi 3:10 sense, by obeying Him in some fresh way. The chapters have been roughly arranged to move from more passive to more active concepts, with the first five topics encouraging the creation of distance from the influences of the world and the latter five encouraging Christians to participate in the world as Christians. All of the concepts are presented in what I hope is a manner that is faithful to the scriptures while considering new angles and approaches that may surprise and challenge you as you read about them and put them into practice.

This book was not intended to offer all the answers but to spur your thinking and investigation of the biblical text. As such, I encourage you to spend time with each topic, read the associated scriptures, and engage in reflection and prayer. **Decide what you will set aside to read, think, pray, and put your insights into action**. Resolve to make room for God as you read and think. My prayer is that it will strengthen your resolve to resist the temptations of this world as you become increasingly alert to and aware of God's presence in your life.

May all God's people live in a way that points others to Christ.

2 Resistance

"For the Christian mind to be truly Christian, there must be room left to challenge systems and structures that would sustain distorted or incomplete accounts of the Christian community's imagined social existence together."
—James Spencer, Thinking Christian4

In the fictional world of Oceania created in George Orwell's 1984, Winston Smith lives under the watchful eye of "Big Brother," who serves as the symbolic head of Oceania's totalitarian regime. Those who hold power in Oceania ("the Party") exert almost complete control over the lives of Oceania's citizens, employing a virtually omnipresent system of monitoring to ensure citizens adhere to the rules of society, employing secret spies to make colluding against "Big Brother" in private more dangerous and difficult, discouraging social interactions, reengineering language, and manipulating history.

Working in the "Ministry of Truth," which concerned itself with news, entertainment, education, and fine arts, Winston participates in the manipulation of history.[5] His job was "to alter, or, as the official phrase had it, to rectify" past reporting that no longer matched (or served) present reality.[6] Winston's role was to secure the Party's control over time because the one "who controls the past…controls the future" and the one "who controls the present controls the past."[7] Despite his "rectifying" work, Winston did not recognize what he did as "forgery" but as "merely the substitution of one piece of nonsense for another.[8] Winston knows there is something rotten in Oceania. He suspects that the world has not been this way forever, yet the past has been, in many cases, erased by his own hand. He longs for something more, yet the mechanisms of control employed by Big Brother and the Party keep him in a state of fear, confusion, and (self-) delusion. He knows what he knows but to express it will bring punishment, or, as Winston comes to understand, *conversion*.

Amid a torturous interrogation, O'Brien, Winston's interrogator, tells Winston that he has not been arrested to be punished, but to be converted. As O'Brien notes:

> "We [the Party] are not content with negative obedience, nor even with the most abject submission. When finally you surrender to us, it must be of your own free will. We do not destroy the heretic because he resists us; so long as he resists us, we never destroy him. We convert him, we capture his inner mind, we reshape him."[9]

In the twisted world of *1984*, resisting the Party cannot be solved through death. It can only be addressed through the reorientation of one's beliefs and commitments so that, in the end, those who once resisted have "nothing left in them except sorrow for what they had done, and love of Big Brother."[10]

As Christians, we live in the midst of fictions that tempt us to live as if God, if He exists at all, is not holy, sovereign, wise, and benevolent. We are tempted to participate in the world as if God is irrelevant. While the mechanisms of control may not be as extreme as Orwell's creations in *1984*, **there is a sense in which the principalities and powers with which we interact press us to "convert" so that we love what they desire us to love in the way they desire us to love it.** Recognizing the principalities and powers reminds us that we are not struggling with "flesh and blood," but with "spiritual forces of evil in the heavenly realms" (Eph 6:12; cf. Col 2:8, 20).

Humans reflect the powers and principalities they serve.[11] While fallen humanity may continue to reflect the image of God in some distorted fashion, the distortions result from delusions. These delusions occur as part of a process of "reciprocal narrowing."[12] Originating within medical literature related to addiction, reciprocal narrowing occurs when we use brain-altering substances (e.g., alcohol, marijuana, etc.) to cope with stressors in our environment. Those substances reduce (or narrow) our ability to perceive the options available to us in a given situation. This reciprocal narrowing continues until we can only respond to the world as "addicts."[13]

This narrowing doesn't necessarily require the use of substances like alcohol or mind-altering drugs. The stories we tell about the world can work in a similar way to the extent that they (a) diminish our cognitive flexibility or ability to think adaptively and (b) reinforce and promote an incomplete view of the world *while presenting that view as complete.*[14] As our perspective on the world narrows, we lose the ability to improvise as God, in His infinite capacity, holds out fresh possibilities for us in the present. The principalities and powers deceive us so that we end up deprioritizing God. As we do so, we increasingly isolate ourselves from Him and begin to lose sight of the possibilities He alone can provide. Our view narrows so much that God appears only at the margins of our vision (if at all), thus weakening our ability to resist through obedience. When God is not at the forefront of our vision, we will find it more difficult to engage in obedient resistance.

As Christians, we commit to a process of discipleship that demands resistance and learning. The two aren't separate activities but work together as we seek to identify the relevant features of our various environments. Our resistance involves refusing to view the world as a closed system in which God is not active and present. We resist the temptation to assume that the possibilities the world offers are the only or most likely possibilities. This form of resistance allows us to remain open to what God, who is capable of doing "far more abundantly than all that we ask or think" (Eph 3:20), is doing in our midst. We are not limited to the options presented by the powers and principalities because they neither speak for God nor desire to enhance our devotion to Him.

Consider, for instance, the temptation of Christ in Matthew 4. Jesus has been fasting for forty days and forty nights (Matt 4:2). Despite His hunger, He resists the temptation to narrow His options down to those presented by "the tempter" (4:3). All three temptations focus on what it means for Christ to be the "Son of God" (4:3, 6). In the first two temptations, the devil tempts Jesus by seeking to limit or define what it means to be the Son of God in terms of the use of power and privilege for one's own advantage and comfort.[15] By starting the first two temptations with the condition "if you are the Son of God," the devil calls Jesus to demonstrate His position as the Son of God by addressing His specific circumstances. Either Jesus narrows His focus to attend to His immediate needs or maintains a broader vision that reflects His trust in God despite His present circumstances (Matt 4:4, 7).[16]

The final temptation is similar, though it does not contain the conditional "If you are the Son of God…" that began in the first two. Instead, the devil offers Christ all the kingdoms of the world in exchange for Christ's worship. Here again, the temptation seeks to limit or narrow what it means to be Christ. Will Jesus inherit all the kingdoms of the world? Yes. Ruling over all things is certainly part of what it means to be Christ, yet Christ's rule cannot come through a backroom deal on a mountaintop. It must be accomplished according to the will of God and through the "cup" of suffering and crucifixion (26:39). It must come through a life lived in full devotion to God the Father, regardless of the difficulties life may bring (4:10).

The powers and principalities desire what God requires: all we are and have (Deut 6:4; Matt 22:37; Lk 10:27). **Resisting the principalities and powers is a matter of loving God without remainder** (cf. 1 Jn 5:2). We resist by refusing to ally ourselves with powers and principalities whose stories deny and diminish God. We, like Christ, refuse to narrow what it means to be human by living as if the powers and principalities and the solutions they present are more relevant than God or take priority over Him. Instead, as we look out upon the landscape of our lives, we recognize the vastness of God, who is unconstrained by the objects we can't move and the forces we can't stop. Through resistance, we remain open to the opportunities only God can provide.

Reflecting on Resistance

Scripture Reading

- Deuteronomy 6:1-9 *be careful to do, it will go well w/ you*
- Deuteronomy 6:10-25 *watch yourself lest, that you dont forget the Lord it will be dangerous*
- Deuteronomy 8:1-20 *promises & warnings*
- Matthew 4:1-11 *temptations of Jesus*
- Hebrews 12:3-11 *donot grow weary - lose heart, see Lord - disciplines*
- 1 Peter 5:6-11 *God is oppose to the proud, gives grace to the humble. Cast all your care on him, resist devil*

Questions

- What am I anxious or fearful of today? Am I concerned about letting others down, looking foolish, failing, or suffering in some way? What conventions or expectations am I allowing to rule in my life?
- How am I allowing the world's stories to capture my attention so that God becomes more peripheral in my vision? When do I tend to put God not in the foreground, but in the background?
- What am I willing to change (specifically) about my life so that I can begin to recognize God's active presence in the world? How can I remove the influences that push God to the margins?

Prayer

- God, I confess that I am too prone not to resist the temptations I encounter. I am too quick to follow the conventions and embrace the possibilities the powers and principalities of this world provide. Their solutions often seem convenient and their promises comfortable. They seem to serve my interests even if only in the short-term. Yet, as I look to my own interests or current circumstances, I narrow my options. Lord, I ask You to direct my affections toward You so that I, like Jesus, can resist the temptation to define myself on my own terms or on the terms of others. Help me resist the world by loving and serving You without reserve or regret despite my present circumstances. Amen.

3 Imitation

"Structural evil may be best understood as a given social configuration or social imaginary constituted by assumptions, habits, cultural practices, policies, or institutions that threaten to conform us (whether individually or collectively) to the image of something other than Christ."
—James Spencer, *Thinking Christian*[17]

In *Deceit, Desire, and the Novel,* René Girard describes the concept of "triangular" or "memetic desire." This desire involves a subject, an object of desire, and a mediator or model whom the subject emulates. Girard argues that instead of focusing solely or even primarily on the relationship between a subject and its object of desire, we should also attend to the dynamics between the subject and model. If we neglect this latter dynamic, we will likely fail to notice that "the impulse toward the object [of desire] is ultimately an impulse toward the mediator."[18]

Girard illustrates this impulse through Don Quixote's admiration for Amadis of Gaul and his commitment to pursue the sort of idyllic chivalry Amadis embodied. As Don Quixote concludes, "I reckon that whoever imitates him [Amadis] best will come closest to perfect chivalry."[19] A number of other commitments cascade from Don Quixote's commitment to imitate Amadis. As Girard argues, "he [Don Quixote] no longer chooses the objects of his own desire—Amadis must choose for him. The disciple pursues objects that are determined for him, or at least seem to be determined for him, by the model of all chivalry."[20]

In the case of Don Quixote, becoming more chivalrous by imitating Amadis seems a virtuous aim; however, much of Girard's work highlights the *potential* for mimetic rivalry as the model becomes an obstacle that the subject feels he must overcome to obtain the object of the subject's desire. It turns out that who we imitate matters. It also turns out that we aren't always as conscious about who we imitate as we might think.

Sociologist Pierre Bourdieu, for instance, posits a series of semi-autonomous fields of competition in which people pursue capitals of various sorts.[21] The quest to be successful in pursuing various forms of capital creates a disposition (habitus) that emerges from a "practical evaluation of the likelihood of the success of a given action in a given situation."[22] At the risk of oversimplifying Bourdieu, the competitive fields we inhabit influence and inform the strategies and personal characteristics we develop to pursue the field-based capital in question. As such, we look to and imitate those individuals, groups, and "fuzzy sets, not checklists, of attributes (e.g., attitudes and behaviors)" that have proven successful in the past.[23] We mimic that which seems to maximize our potential in a particular field's capital.

As an illustration, consider a three-hundred-fifty-pound individual attempting to choose between becoming an NFL lineman and pursuing the ballet. Assuming that the individual is athletic, is it more likely that they would succeed in becoming a defensive tackle or the lead in Swan Lake? Given that both are possible, the NFL lineman track seems more likely. That isn't to say there are no anomalies. Height, for instance, is one factor in making it to the NBA, but Mugsy Bogues, the shortest player in NBA history, had a fifteen-year career as a point guard at five feet, three inches. Still, habitus is not about anomalies but norms or likelihoods. Could a 350-pound individual be a ballet dancer? It may be possible, but it isn't likely. Given those who have achieved success in the past, the characteristics associated with success in the two sports appear to differ. Recognizing that ballet dancers tend to be relatively small whereas linemen tend to be relatively large, is part of the habitus that emerges in the "practical evaluation of the likelihood of the success of a given action in a given situation."[24]

The point is that we tend to mimic not only individuals but prototypes or profiles. Like Don Quixote, we see in these prototypes idealized embodiments of certain characteristics that we seek to imitate. The person or people we seek to imitate align, to some significant degree, with some goal or aim we have come to understand as important. To achieve that goal, it often seems that one must muster the strength that comes from the accumulation of various forms of capital. As such, we look to those who have accumulated capital and begin to imitate them so that we can attain the desired object. We come to define ourselves, in some non-trivial sense, according to the models we seek to imitate.

By modeling our lives after those who have achieved some earthly success, we run the risk of becoming successful ourselves. I say "run the risk" because success, when understood in terms of wealth or worldly status, can be deformative. Success can be deformative in so much as it requires the setting aside of faithful obedience. When we are willing to allow something other than Christ to determine our desires, we do not imitate Him. Instead, we reproduce through imitation a form of life patterned on distorted images of God that are unformed by the revelation of God in Christ.

In 1 Corinthians 11:1, Paul concludes his discussion of Christian action by exhorting the believers in Corinth to "Be imitators of me, as I am of Christ." His exhortation is preceded by a series of discussions related to realities and rights, particularly with regard to food sacrificed to idols. His argument begins by affirming that idols are nothing (8:4) and that "food will not commend us to God" (8:8). Yet, while eating food sacrificed to idols has no effect on those who "possess knowledge" (8:1; 8:7), it can have a detrimental effect on those with a weak conscience who will eat the food "as really offered to an idol" (8:7). It is possible that by eating food sacrificed to idols, those with knowledge will end up "sinning against your brothers and wounding their conscience when it is weak" and, thus, "sin against Christ" (8:12).

Having stated that if it causes a brother to stumble, he will never eat meat (8:13), Paul goes on to list the various rights he has already set aside (9:1–7). He has the right to marry, yet he remains single (9:5). He has the right to be supported in the ministry, yet he works for a living (9:6–12). Still, Paul has set aside his rights to avoid putting "an obstacle in the way of the gospel of Christ" (9:12). Paul seeks to be "all things to all people, that by all means I might save some" (9:22). Paul is not advocating that we adopt a stance of unrestrained relativism that denies the truth but rather a selfless posture in which we no longer pursue our rights at any cost. We, like Christ, do not see what God has given us as something to be used to our own advantage (Phil 2:6), but to be given away as an act of selfless love for others.

While Paul may appear to have given the Corinthians license to eat food sacrificed to idols, his discussion in 10:1-22 reveals that in addition to his desire to guard those with a weak conscience, he also desires those who possess the knowledge to avoid idolatry. Despite their shared baptism and spiritual food and drink, God was displeased with most of the Israelites in the wilderness (10:1–5). Rather than express their loyalty and gratitude through obedience, many of the Israelites engaged in idolatry and sexual immorality (10:6–10). Paul desires the Corinthians to avoid this mistake and, thus, urges them to "flee from idolatry" highlighting that one cannot partake in the Lord's Supper and, at the same time, participate in meals where demons are worshiped (10:14–22).

Paul goes on to suggest that while all things are "lawful... not all things are helpful" (10:23). The Corinthians are not to become obsessed with the origins or histories of the food they eat (10:25–27), yet if they become aware that what they are eating has been sacrificed to an idol, they should abstain "for the sake of the one who informed you" (10:28). Nothing has changed about the meat, nor is Paul suggesting that idols are "anything" (10:19–20). Instead, Paul encourages the Corinthians to imitate Christ by setting aside their "own good" to pursue "the good of their neighbor" (10:24). It is in our willingness to set aside our rights and the blessings God has given us to serve our neighbor that we imitate Christ.

Christ becomes the model we seek to imitate. As we imitate Him, our relationship with the objects around us is transformed. If, like Christ, we do not see our rights, talents, or blessings as tools to be used for our own advantage because "self-giving love" is "the true mark of the life of the Spirit." As we imitate Christ through self-giving love, we will begin to recognize that our environment affords us opportunities to love God and our neighbor. If, as Girard suggests, we opt to surrender our desires and adopt those of our model, we will increasingly find that we are more interested in the building up of the body of Christ and the salvation of the lost than we are with our own prosperity and abundance. As such, discipleship, or the process by which we learn to mimic Christ in our day-to-day lives, is required if God's people are to care for one another or have a passion for the unsaved.

To put it differently, if we are to "walk properly as in the daytime, not in orgies and drunkenness, not in sexual immorality and sensuality, not in quarreling and jealousy" (Rom 13:13), we must renovate our desires by committing to be disciples of Christ. In discipleship, we commit to allowing Christ to determine our desires so that being like Him becomes the driving force of our lives. As disciples, we do not always imitate Christ because we see clearly how doing so will bring about a specific outcome. In fact, one of the dangers of having our own agendas, measures of success, or legitimate concerns involves the potential for them to overshadow our desire to imitate Christ so that we opt into what we deem practical or urgent. Imitating Christ involves adopting a logic that is only available to those who believe in Christ's bodily resurrection and subsequent glorification, through which God vindicated Christ's way of life and being in the world. When we imitate Christ, we may find ourselves, like the Son of Man, with nowhere to lay our heads (Matt 8:20). Even so, we can be sure that according to the logic that leads to resurrection, glorification, and life in the presence of God in the new heavens and the new earth (Rev 21:1).

Reflecting on Imitation

Scripture Reading

- 1 Corinthians 8:1–13
- 1 Corinthians 9:1–27
- 1 Corinthians 10:1–22
- 1 Corinthians 10:23–11:1
- Matthew 8:18–22
- Revelation 21:1-8

Questions

- How am I imitating Christ in my daily life currently?
- What desires are overshadowing my desire to follow Christ in all things?
- To what extent am I trying to make Jesus look more like me because of my unwillingness to set aside my agendas, legitimate concerns, strategies, or moral outrage?
- How committed am I to being a disciple of Christ rather than being a "good" or "moral" person? What is the difference?

Prayer

- Lord, you have revealed yourself to us in your word and your Son. You have called us to be disciples and to make disciples. Help me commit to imitating Christ. Show me those areas where I am unwilling to be self-giving. Identify those desires I am unwilling to leave behind. Let me fix my eyes on Christ, emulate Him, and allow my desires to be reshaped so that I may increase in faithfulness and point others to You. Amen.

4 Time

"We need a space to have the sort of slow, deliberate dialogues that reflect our deep conviction that discerning the Spirit is crucial to offering faithful testimony."[25]
—James Spencer, *Thinking Christian*

Time is one of the most valuable resources that many of us waste. In part, time is easy to waste because we don't understand how we relate to it and, thus, are unsure of how to use it wisely. As we think about time, however, we will quickly realize that, when wielded well, it is one of the most powerful tools God has given us to serve him. As Christians learn to use time well, we will increasingly learn to remember God in the midst of a broken world.

Our Relation to Time

In his essay titled, "A Definition of the Concept of History," historian Johan Huizinga suggests, "Every man renders account to himself of the past in accordance with the standards which his education and *Weltanschauung* [worldview] lead him to adopt."[26] In this description, Huizinga makes an important connection between the past and the present. The stream of information (and our interpretation of it) does not simply run from "then to now," but from "now to then." Moreover, both the past and the present gesture toward, and are informed by, our hoped-for future.

Past, present, and future offer helpful ways for us to think about time. The past represents where we have been. The present approximates where we are.[27] And the future is about where we anticipate going. As helpful as this threefold division of time is, our experience of time is a bit more complex because we tend to give the past, present, and future relevance by prioritizing certain events over others. As such, we can think about our relation to time through two additional categories: accessibility and influence.

When we think about time, we recognize that we are unaware of everything occurring in the past or the present. Much of the past and present are *not* accessible to us. For instance, prior to their discovery in the 1970s, the Dead Sea Scrolls were not accessible to us. They could not be factored into our understanding of the scriptures because, at the time, they were a part of the past to which we were not privy. Once made accessible, the Dead Sea Scrolls became relatively *influential.*

Accessibility does not always result in influence. For instance, barring food poisoning or some allergic reaction, knowing what I had for lunch yesterday isn't particularly consequential to my life. It is almost certainly inconsequential to your life. I could tell you that I had fish tacos, and it would not impact your life in the least (unless, of course, you now have a craving for fish tacos). The point is that much of the accessible information exists on a continuum of importance ranging from the utterly trivial (what I had for lunch) to the absolutely crucial (the bodily resurrection of Christ).

Of all that is accessible to us (in the past and the present), we determine what will *influence* our way of thinking and being in the world. We decide which stories, ideas, facts, etc., will contribute to what philosopher Charles Taylor calls our "social imaginary."[28] Our social imaginary is "something much broader and deeper than the intellectual schemes people may entertain when they think about social reality in a disengaged mode."[29] Instead, it involves "the ways people imagine their social existence, how they fit together with others, how things go on between them and their fellows, the expectations that are normally met, and the deeper normative notions and images that underlie these expectations."[30]

As we determine what is and is not influential, we begin to engage in practices that reflect our understanding of the past and the present. These practices are often a matter of remembering or reconstructing the past in the present.[31] As we "re-member" or reconstruct the past in the present, we engage in a rather complex activity of interpretation as we decide how to make sense of the world that confronts us.

This process isn't always improvisational (though it can be). Often, we are more intentional about our remembering. For instance, we engage in ongoing rituals and reenactments of some crucial past events. Rituals are "memory-inducing behavior that has the effect of preserving what is indispensable to the group" in the present and beyond.[32] These memory-inducing behaviors are not limited to religious groups but are used by the various other groups of which we are a part. For instance, dining the national anthem at sporting events is a non-religious ritual symbolizing some level of solidarity with a notion of what it means to be a citizen of the United States. While it may be tempting to dismiss such rituals as ineffective, consider the controversy brought on when various professional athletes opted out of the ritual by kneeling rather than standing. The disruption of the ritual was not trivial because it called into question the coherence of the story normally assumed by the ritual. In inducing particular sorts of memory, the world's rituals press us to consider indispensable what is, in reality, dispensable. As such, part of our Christian resistance involves the development of a rhythm of life within time that reminds us that God is present and active among us.[33]

Using Time Wisely

When viewed as (a) a process of reconstruction and interpretation toward sense-making that employs aspects of the past and present and (b) a space punctuated if not structured by ritual, our relationship to time and interaction with it becomes quite important. The rituals we engage in and the portions of the past that we identify as influential in the present will condition the way we think and act.

As Christians, we recognize the Bible as part of the past that is *always and ultimately* relevant in the present. It is the "living and active" Word of God that endures and offers timeless wisdom (Heb 4:12; 1 Pet 1:23–25; 2 Tim 3:16). The practices of the church, such as the Lord's Supper, point us back to Christ's sacrifice and our union with Him. Even our celebration of holidays or use of the church calendar creates a cadence of life that reminds us of our place in God's world.

Still, we are also living under the influence of other rituals. Rituals are not habits because, in general, habits are not memory-inducing. Instead, rituals normally involve some group activities that reinforce group belonging by (a) highlighting some shared experience and (b) triggering a similar emotional response from all participants. These rituals bring people together and provide a shared sense of the past and present. Christian rituals allow God's people to demonstrate a way of reckoning time that looks past death. Such a reckoning is perhaps most evident in the lives of martyrs. God's people have the opportunity to live according to "the eschatological imagination," which "sees that, although they presume to kill us, Christ has vanquished the powers of death once and for all."[34]

We relate to time through memory to some significant degree. As such, we must take care to structure our rituals in ways that help us remember God as "whoever raised Jesus from the dead, having before raised Israel from Egypt."[35] To put it differently, as we relate to the past, present, and future, we, as Christians, not only recognize the Bible as the final authority for life and faith, but we also live according to a rhythm of life, punctuated and structured by rituals that remind us we are in Christ. As such, we can understand what it means to "share His [Christ's] sufferings" (Phil 3:10) as more than a simple analogy. It is a present reality in which the innocent suffering and rejection of our Savior are replayed in our lives. Our lives, in some sense, become ritual acts (a) pointing back in time to the life, death, and resurrection of Christ and (b) pointing toward what it means to look forward to the new creation as we walk in the newness of life.

Our time is spent wisely to the extent that we not only reserve time for God but use our time in such a way that worship of God becomes as natural as breathing. As Old Testament scholar Deryck Sherriffs notes, "Intensity of experience means that the mind fills with phrases from Israel's repertoire of prayer on waking up in the morning, whether the mood on awakening is one of desperation or delight."[36] Time is the gift God has given us to become people who remember Him. It is the context in which we demonstrate what is most important to us. We use time wisely by meditating on God's instruction day and night (Ps 1:2), recognizing His fresh mercies every morning (Lam 3:22–23), and doing good rather than harm all the days of our lives (Prov 31:12). Time is the arena in which we experience God so that we may boast in our knowledge and understanding of Him (Jer 9:24).).

Reflecting on Time

Scripture Reading

- Psalm 1
- Jeremiah 9:12-26
- Lamentations 3:1-27
- Philippians 2:1-29
- Philippians 3:1-10

Questions

- How does the way I am using my time reflect what is truly important to me?
- What is one step I can take to begin developing a rhythm in my daily life that will make worshiping God throughout the day as natural as breathing?
- What are some past experiences or information about the past that I view as most influential? Why?

Prayer

- God, when You created the world, You created day and night. You instituted time. You made the seasons, established Sabbath, instituted festivals, and encouraged Your people to live so as to remember, honor, and glorify You in their daily lives. Thank You for the gift of time. Help me today not to waste time. It is a gift from You and not something to be carelessly spent on my own agendas or worries. Each and every moment of each and every day is another opportunity for me to experience Your ongoing presence in my life. Time offers me the opportunity to point others to You. Show me how I have been wasting time and give me the wisdom to use it more wisely. Amen.

5 Response

"Distraction leads us to react and respond. It cultivates a sense of urgency...a sense that if we do not act, we will surrender ground that we cannot win back...the distractions begin to become our reality."
—James Spencer, *Thinking Christian*[37]

As Christians, we affirm God's omnipresence. God is present and active in the world. Affirming that God is everywhere and experiencing God's presence in a given moment is not trivial because "The divine presence of which we can be aware is always particular."[38] Accepting that God is present everywhere *in the abstract* doesn't necessarily mean that we live as if He is present with us at any given moment. Yet, if God is present, shouldn't it impact the way we live our lives at every given moment?

Assuming that God's presence *should* influence us, we can begin to consider *how* it should influence us. Understanding how God's presence influences our daily lives requires that we learn to fear God. Fearing the Lord is a matter of responding to God with obedience because we recognize that (a) God deserves our loyalty and (b) trusting in anyone or anything other than God is futile. As Old Testament scholar Bruce Waltke notes regarding Israel, "For them, the fear of I Am is just as real as their love for him. Both psyches are rooted in their faith: they believe his promises and love him; they believe his threats and fear him."[39] This is the essence of what it means to fear the Lord: **we recognize God's presence**

in our midst and respond first and foremost to Him rather than to the people and circumstances we encounter.

God's presence and willingness to be with and for the people of Israel conditioned how the Israelites treated one another. In Leviticus, God offers a series of commands to Israel, all of which are rooted in this notion of God-fearing. The deaf and blind may not be able to defend against curses and stumbling blocks, but God can and will (Lev 19:14). Injustice, poor treatment of neighbors, selfishness, and other actions that disadvantage others are precluded because "I am the Lord" (Lev 19:10, 12, 14, 16, 18).

Beyond prohibitions, God's law also points toward the empowerment God provides to allow us to respond to Him in obedience. For instance, God commands Israel to take a year of Jubilee in which they are not to "sow or gather" (Lev 25:20) any crop. God promises to "command my blessing on you in the sixth year, so that it [the land] will produce a crop sufficient for three years" (25:21). The year of Jubilee is made possible by God's promise and blessing. As Israel responds with obedience to God, they will move beyond the affirmation that God exists and toward an experience of His presence as they see Him do as He said He would.

The Israelites were to live in the light of God's presence. They were not to live as if God was not there with them but to orient their whole lives around Him. Like Israel, when we recognize "the Lord's awesome power and majesty clearly before us, we are quick to obey him, holding fast to his life-giving paths as we bow in reverential worship before our heavenly King."[40] When we recognize that God is particularly present in our midst, we have little choice but to respond with obedience.

An obedient response does not always correlate to immediate action. At times, obeying God requires restraint and patience. For instance, when Moses kills an Egyptian who is oppressing a Hebrew, he does so in response to the immediate situation. Yet, his action cannot bring about a change in the state of things. By responding to the situation rather than responding to God within the situation, Moses takes matters into his own hands and ends up being forced to flee to Midian. Only God could liberate Israel from Egypt in a way that would result in Israel being a "kingdom of priests and a holy nation" (Exod 19:6).[41] **No human action could ever free Israel from the oppressive weight of a broken world that too often demands unceasing labor, precludes love of neighbor, and squeezes out worship.**

Responding to God is not something we learn without trial and error. Still, we should seek to avoid what historian Mark Noll refers to as "an immediatism that insists on action, decision, and even perfection *right now*."[42] Learning to respond to God rather than the situation will require repentance and confession, as well as learning to look past the outcomes we achieve to consider the process that we followed to achieve them. Like the tower builders of Babel, we have the capacity to do a great deal without God. We can only hope that God intervenes to redirect our path and keep us from building a tower and a city apart from Him (Gen 11:6–7).

Jacob provides another example of responding to the situation rather than responding to God within the situation. Upon hearing that Esau is traveling to meet him, Jacob divides his camp so that at least a portion of his party might escape if Esau attacks (Gen 32:6–8). Jacob has been waiting a long time for the blessing he received from his father Isaac (27:1–46). Since his dream at Bethel, Jacob has been waiting for God to fulfill His promise to give him land and offspring (28:13–15). Now, after fleeing Laban, to whom he was obligated for more than a decade, he must face yet another uncertain challenge. While he prays for God's deliverance, he is not at peace. After sending his wives across the Jabbok, Jacob wrestles with God, who touches his hip so that it goes out of joint (32:22–32).

This final event, in which Jacob wrestles with God and has his hip socket dislocated, has a restraining effect on Jacob. His frenzied attempts to proactively appease Esau are ultimately unnecessary, as he must convince Esau to keep the gifts he has offered (33:10–11). Now, Jacob's desire to receive God's blessing seems surer than ever. Traveling with Esau is the quicker and perhaps safer path, yet Jacob's hip will only allow him to move at the pace of the children and the flocks (33:34). By injuring his hip, God slows Jacob down. God limits him so that Jacob can no longer move at a frenzied pace and must exercise restraint. Jacob could no longer respond as he might have to the situations he encounters and is now left to respond to God as he moves more slowly through life.

Responding to God rather than responding to a situation requires discernment. When we see injustice, pain, or other forms of brokenness, it is tempting for us to act in our own strength. We tend to follow our intuition rather than taking the time to think and pray, *not* about how to address the situation, but about how God desires us to walk in obedience given the situation. **Seeking to respond to God will not leave Christians inactive**. Instead, it will allow Christians to be directed to act in ways that demonstrate God's active presence in our midst to a broken world.

King David offers a wonderful example of the sort of deliberation necessary to respond to God rather than responding to a situation. After David is anointed king of Israel, he is pursued by Saul, who remains on the Israelite throne (1 Sam 24:1-2). While hiding in a cave, David and his men are confronted with an opportunity to kill Saul, who has entered the cave to relieve himself (24:3). David's men urge David to kill Saul, saying, "Here is the day of which the Lord said to you, 'Behold, I will give your enemy into your hand, and you shall do to him as it shall seem good to you'" (24:4). Yet, after cutting off a corner of Saul's robe, David realizes that he and his men cannot raise a hand against Saul, "seeing he [Saul] is the Lord's anointed" (24:6). David does not let the situation he is in determine the course of his actions. Instead, he entrusts himself to God (24:8–15) and refuses to take matters into his own hands.

Learning to respond obediently to God rather than responding to the opportunities and urgencies of the moment is no simple matter. It requires patience, trust, and surrendering control. It is often uncomfortable to wait (even for God) in light of the difficulties confronting us. Yet, as Christians, we must learn to respond to God because, as Dwight Moody rightly notes, "I cannot look into the future. I do not know what is going to happen tomorrow; in fact, I do not know what may happen before night; so, I cannot choose for myself as well as God can choose for me, and it is much better to surrender my will to God's will."[43]

Reflecting on Response

Scripture Reading

- Genesis 11:1-9
- Genesis 32:1-33:20
- Exodus 2:11-25
- Leviticus 19:9-17
- 1 Samuel 24:1-22

Questions

- How will what I am doing (or thinking of doing) point others to Christ?
- As I look back on my day, how much did I accomplish without God?
- At what point(s) during my day did I take the time to think, study, or pray about how best to respond to God rather than a situation I was facing?

Prayer

- Lord, I desire to respond to You today. Give me eyes that see and ears that hear so that I can recognize Your active presence in my life. Help me to look beyond the situations I face. Help me set aside my tendency to do what I can rather than waiting for You to do what You will. Give me the grace to move slower, to be more patient, and to allow the urgencies, anxieties, and frustrations of daily life in a broken world to become light and momentary in comparison to Your glory and power. Thank You, Lord, for calling me from darkness to light through the life, death, and resurrection of Christ. Help me now to walk in the newness of life as I seek to honor You and point others to You. Amen.

6 Attention

"We enjoy our distractions and our distractions (at least some of them) are changing the way we interact with the world around us."
—James Spencer, Thinking Christian[44]

As a Gen X'er born in 1977, I still remember a time when we were less immersed in media. In some significant sense, it was more difficult to get information or view entertainment. For instance, if you wanted to see a particular television show and you didn't have a VCR (or couldn't figure out how to set it to record), you had to plan to be home at a particular time. With the creation of streaming services and digital recording and storage, content is now available on demand. Those who want our attention have made it easy for us to consume content by making it available at any time.

Because we no longer have to be at a certain place at a certain time to consume content, we have the opportunity to watch *more*. We can choose to binge-watch a Netflix series whenever we would like. We can replay Monday Night Football or catch up on the highlights on YouTube TV. We can even consume content that we wouldn't otherwise choose to consume if we had to choose between it and something else that happened to be on at the same time. Add to that the ease with which we can watch, scroll, text, and surf all at the same time, and it seems rather evident that we are now living in a world designed to capture our attention.

Information is not only readily available but also more easily produced and distributed. The frequency with which "new" information is presented is staggering. While the internet and social media are often viewed as the main culprits, broadcast media cannot be ignored. Twenty-four-hour news stations tend to create, as opposed to report, news just as much as the so-called journalists on social media. We are inundated with "urgent" messages and captivated by stories with more sizzle than steak. We are subjected to "what if" reporting that offers hypotheticals because the events of the day aren't interesting enough to hold our attention.

As our attention goes, so goes our perspective of the world. For instance, Chapman University's study of American fears notes a rather strong relationship between the frequency of certain types of media (i.e., liberal or conservative) consumed and the level of fear reported. The fears tended to be correlated with that type of media. Those who watched a conservative news outlet like Fox News on a daily basis reported being afraid of "three times as many conservative political concerns ['Obamacare, gun control, illegal immigrants'] compared to someone who never does."[45] Those who watch more liberal news outlets like MSNBC on a daily basis report being "fearful of almost twice as many of these [liberal] concerns ['Trumpcare, white supremacists, anti-immigrant groups, sovereign citizens, and extreme anti-tax groups'] compared to those who never watch MSNBC."[46] As the news captures our attention, it also shapes our perspective.[47]

Media, particularly media delivered by technologies within the attention economy, selects, propagates, and interprets information to compete for our attention.[48] Competition suggests that something of value is up for grabs. In this case, it is our attention. It is clear that a variety of businesses, influencers, media outlets, etc., are competing for our attention. As a matter of Christian resistance, we need to be competing *for our own attention* in the sense that we want to attend in ways that direct us toward that which has true, eternal value. We want (or should want) to attend to God and His Kingdom. We are competing to direct our attention so that God becomes particularly noticeable or salient. We want God to have our attention because He is infinitely more prominent in any situation than anything else to which we might attend.

When we attend to something, we recognize its relevance.[49] We prioritize one thing over another by the way we allocate our attention. When we allocate our attention, we can diminish God's salience, or particular relevance, in our everyday lives from moment to moment. We give God less attention and, thus, a lower priority. We give our attention to the most important aspects of our lives. When social media and news outlets seek to direct our attention, they aren't simply seeking to monetize our views and clicks in the short term **but to own our attention so that we come to believe that what they say is the most relevant thing that could be said.** To put it differently, those who compete for our attention want to steer our attention continually; however, in a market economy, we must take care to remember that we are not without responsibility. They sell. We buy. In doing so, we agree with the world that God, if He exists at all, is less prominent than the scriptures suggest. We allow God to fade into the background as we give other aspects of our environment pride of place.

For instance, consider the assessment of the land that the spies (except Caleb and Joshua) bring back to Moses and the people in the book of Numbers. Some spies recognize the beauty and prosperity of the land but see the inhabitants as a threat because "we seemed to ourselves like grasshoppers, and so we seemed to them" (Num 13:33). The other spies can't see past the challenges that exist in the land because "the people who dwell in the land are strong, and cities are fortified and very large" (13:28). This bad, though not false, report wreaks havoc among the people by focusing their attention on the strength of those who dwell in the land and the relative lack of strength Israel has to overcome them. The people of the land quickly become more relevant than God, so the people ask, "Why is the Lord bringing us into this land, to fall by the sword?" (14:3).

In juxtaposition, Caleb, who has seen everything the spies have seen, is prepared to enter the land despite the strength of its inhabitants (13:30). After the Israelites consider choosing a new leader to take them back to Egypt (14:4), Joshua and Caleb, who were among those who spied out the land, remind the people that it is not their strength that will overcome the inhabitants of the land, but God's strength: "If the Lord delights in us, he will bring us into this land and give it to us, a land that flows with milk and honey. Only do not rebel against the Lord. And do not fear the people of the land, for they are bread for us. Their protection is removed from them, and the Lord is with us; do not fear them" (14:8–9).

The spies' report is not false on its face, but it is delivered from a particular point of view. The spies interpret what they have seen and assign relevance to it. They pay more attention to what they see than to the fact that God is with them. As such, they prioritize the size and strength of the people in the land and deprioritize God. The spies aren't lying about what they saw. *They are attending wrongly.*

The people of Israel also give their attention to the disparity between themselves and the inhabitants of the land. In doing so, they relegate all God has done to the background (14:11). They refuse to see God as the most relevant factor in their situation. With God, as Joshua and Caleb urged, taking the land is simply a matter of time (14:8–9). Joshua and Caleb are not primarily attending to what they have seen in the land but to their experience and understanding of God. God is the most relevant factor. For Joshua and Caleb, the inhabitants fade into irrelevance because God has captured their attention. Who God is determines their understanding of the situation in which they find themselves.

Like Jesus, we do not look past the troubles we face in this world (Matt 26:39; Lk 22:42). We look to the pattern of Christ, "who for the joy that was set before him endured the cross, despising the shame, and is seated at the right hand of the throne of God" (Heb 12:2). Jesus was aware of what He would suffer as "his sweat became like great drops of blood" at the Mount of Olives (Lk 22:44), yet His attention remained on the Father. Even in His darkest moment, Jesus' cry is not about the pains of crucifixion (of which there were surely many) but about the Father's absence (Matt 27:46).[50] Recognizing that God has given Him over to suffering and will not intervene, Jesus, whose attention had been focused on the Father, now attends to the Father's absence and the horrors of facing a broken world without God.

As we attend to God, we will experience reality at a deeper level. We won't ignore our circumstances. We will put them in their proper place under

God. That to which we would have devoted our attention and deemed most relevant without God, we will begin to see with new eyes as we focus our attention on the Master and look to imitate those who follow His ways (Phil 3:17).

Reflecting on Attention

Scripture Reading

- Numbers 13-14
- Matthew 27:1-56
- Matthew 27:57-28:20
- Luke 22:39-46
- Philippians 3:12-21
- Hebrews 12:1-17

Questions

- What are the primary contenders for my attention?
- Do I interpret the situations in which I find myself as if God is present? Do I see the challenges I face in light of God's sovereignty, wisdom, and benevolence?
- Would I notice if God was absent?

Prayer

- Lord, there are many things in this world that compete for my attention. I'm often drawn to the sensational stories and urgencies of the day. I'm often too prone to believe those who interpret the world as if You were not in it. I allow my attention to drift away from You so that You are no longer in the foreground but in the background. Help me to remain attentive to You. Show me how to attend to Your presence so that I know I am not alone as I face the challenges of this life. You have not forsaken me, but I have too often lost sight of You as my attention drifts away from Christ and those who walk in his ways and toward those who don't know You. Give me the grace and discipline to pay attention to You regardless of the circumstances I face. Amen.

7 Coordination

"The church…is a coordinated, connected community with a peculiar character and mission accomplished by individual and collective acting and speaking within the world for the glory of God."
—James Spencer, Thinking Christian[51]

Sometime last year I was listening to a sermon on freedom. At one point, the pastor referenced the banning of school-sponsored prayer in public schools resulting from the 1962 Supreme Court decision in Engel v. Vitale.[52] Lamenting the loss of the practice, the pastor went on to connect the court's decision to the erosion of the freedom of religion in the United States. "With the prayer ban," he suggested, "Christian freedom had been effectively curtailed."

Whatever opinion you may hold about the U.S. Supreme Court's decision in Engel v. Vitale, President Kennedy's response to the decision is revealing:

> "…we have in this case a very easy remedy and that is to pray ourselves. And I would think it would be a welcome reminder to every American family that we can pray a deal more at home, we can attend our churches with a good deal more fidelity, and we can make the true meaning of prayer much more important in the lives of all of our children. That power is very much open to us."[53]

Here, President Kennedy makes a valid point. Prayer may continue. Yet, while focusing on prayer, he misses a more crucial, underlying problem of the church's coordination.

Engel v. Vitale didn't negate prayer. It made prayer private. It relocated the responsibility for prayer to Christians and the church. Perhaps the most significant aspect of Engel v. Vitale is not the loss of rights or the weakening moral resolve of the United States but the revelation that the church had, to some significant degree, been relying on the state to coordinate public religious activities.[54]

If there is no prayer in public schools today, it says as much, if not more, about the church as it does about the United States government. While Kennedy is certainly correct that prayer at home and (I would add) prayer at church are crucial, these were and are not "a very easy remedy" to what was lost in Engel v. Vitale.[55] They are not "a very easy remedy" because what was revealed in Engel v. Vitale was not the anti-Christian sentiments of the state but that God's people did not have the common knowledge or coordination sufficient to engage in the practice of prayer in the context of public schools *without school sponsorship.*

Engel v. Vitale was a defining moment in the relationship between the United States and religious groups, particularly Christians. It was a reminder that, regardless of past Christian influences, the United States was constitutional, not Christian.[56] At this defining moment, the church *could* have recognized something about itself as well, namely, that by entrusting the state with preserving a religious, if not Christian, context was not only tenuous but detrimental to the body of Christ. By entrusting the state in this way, the church's ability to cultivate common knowledge and to coordinate citizens, even Christian citizens, around the gospel in the public square atrophied.[57]

Coordination is assumed to be an activity in which a given individual desires to participate when a critical mass of other people is also participating. Coordination problems arise because participating individuals must have "knowledge of others' knowledge, knowledge of others' knowledge of others' knowledge, and so on—that is 'common knowledge'."[58] Knowing that there is a critical mass of other people and that those people will be participating in the activity in question requires communication, a shared understanding of that communication, and, usually, some evidence that we are not alone in the tasks we only want to participate in when others are participating with us.

Arguably, the church's ability to coordinate its congregants against society has declined over the years. Something as simple as having youth sporting events on Sunday mornings gestures toward the coordination problems in the church. While growing up, it was common knowledge (in the sense noted above) that Sunday mornings were for worship. Even if people were not practicing Christians, there seemed to be an understanding that Sunday would be a poor day for youth sports because the Christian families would be in church. Today, youth sports are frequently held for the whole weekend or require travel that would make it difficult to be home on a Sunday morning to attend church.

Clearly, as a Christian parent, I could make the individual choice not to allow my children to participate in sports that have games on Sunday or not to participate on Sundays. Still, that decision isn't easy on an individual level. In part, it is difficult because of the lack of common knowledge among Christians regarding the importance of communal worship.[59] In part, it is because I'm sentimental, and, as theologian Stanley Hauerwas puts it, "The great enemy of the church today is not atheism but sentimentality; and there's no deeper sentimentality than the presumption by Christians and nonbelievers alike that they should be able to have children without their children suffering for their convictions."[60] In any case, the church and its members have not coordinated well enough that it becomes easy for individual Christians to do the right thing. Instead, we have too often tended to look to the government or some other organization to preserve the space necessary to practice our faith.

I am not suggesting that God's people are never coordinated. Instead, I am proposing that when the church entrusts other entities (e.g., the government, community groups, professional associations, etc.) to coordinate Christian practices or, as in the case of Sunday morning sports, to coordinate in ways that respect Christian practices, we put too much trust in organizations and people **who have no vested interest in making disciples for Jesus Christ**. Viewed from this perspective, the church's coordination problem could have been anticipated *before* banning school-sponsored prayer because prayer was not a church-sponsored but a school-sponsored activity. Our coordination problems continue to be evident today, as the church's common biblical and theological knowledge is often overshadowed by the issues of the day. However appropriate it may be to address the issues of the day; the church must take care not to prioritize political participation over discipleship.[61]

The church persists not because of any particular arrangement with the state but because of God. Christian coordination is one of the non-negotiables of the faith because we are saved individuals who have been united with Christ and one another to demonstrate the "manifold wisdom of God" to the "rulers and authorities in the heavenly places" (Eph 3:10). We point to Christ as individuals, but we also point to Him together. As such, we have to be together in physical assembly (Heb 13:2) and single-minded solidarity (Phil 1:27; 2:2, 5). As individuals, we must trust that others know Christ and that they will act with us in ways that build the body of Christ and help to coordinate its members.

While I believe Christians can and should do more to coordinate with one another, I also believe that we will often find ourselves in situations where we must *assume* coordination. We must assume that God is raising up others who are disciples and making disciples. That assumption is rooted in our understanding of and trust in God's Word rather than our experience of others in the world. As Elijah lamented being the only one left who has not forsaken God's covenant, we may often feel alone in the practice of our faith (1 Kgs 19:10). Yet, Elijah was not alone. He struggled against the Baals with the "seven thousand in Israel, all the knees that have not bowed to Baal, and every mouth that has not kissed him" (19:18).

In some sense, assuming coordination by living faithfully regardless of the consequences is as important as encouraging coordination through other means. By living under the authority of scripture, we acknowledge God's wisdom and coordinate with other members of Christ's body, *even if we don't know we are doing so*. As such, our essential contribution to the coordination of the church involves becoming "doers of the word" (Jam 1:22) so that we, along with all those who sit under the authority of God's

Word, may be coordinated by God according to His good purpose.

Reflecting on Coordination

Scripture Reading

- Numbers 13-14
- Matthew 27:1-56
- Matthew 27:57-28:20
- Luke 22:39-46
- Philippians 3:12-21
- Hebrews 12:1-17

Questions

- What are the primary contenders for my attention?
- Do I interpret the situations in which I find myself as if God is present? Do I see the challenges I face in light of God's sovereignty, wisdom, and benevolence?
- Would I notice if God was absent?

Prayer

- Lord, there are many things in this world that compete for my attention. I'm often drawn to the sensational stories and urgencies of the day. I'm often too prone to believe those who interpret the world as if You were not in it. I allow my attention to drift away from You so that You are no longer in the foreground but in the background. Help me to remain attentive to You. Show me how to attend to Your presence so that I know I am not alone as I face the challenges of this life. You have not forsaken me, but I have too often lost sight of You as my attention drifts away from Christ and those who walk in His ways and toward those who don't know You. Give me the grace and discipline to pay attention to You regardless of the circumstances I face. Amen.

8 Preservation

"The challenge for the body of Christ is to avoid preoccupations with finite structures that will end. Allowing inertia to propel an organization or institution forward even when God's blessing is no longer upon it does not serve the body of Christ."
—James Spencer, Thinking Christian[62]

In his July 2022 sermon titled "America is a Christian Nation," Robert Jeffress, senior pastor of First Baptist Dallas, presented evidence of Christianity's influence during the founding of the United States. His message, however, sought to do more than remind people of the role Christians, the Christian faith, and even the Bible played in the early days of our nation. It sought to map out a process by which America might continue to enjoy prosperity and progress.

For instance, toward the end of his message, Jeffress quotes former Chief Justice of the Supreme Court, Earl Warren, who made the following remarks at a prayer breakfast in 1954:

> "I believe no one can read the history of the country without realizing that the good book and the spirit of the Savior have from the beginning been our guiding geniuses...I believe the entire Bill of Rights came into being because of the knowledge our forefathers had of the Bible and their belief in it...I like to believe we are living today in the spirit of the Christian religion. I like also to believe that as long as we do so, no great harm can come to our country."[63]

Jeffress follows Warren's quote with the following assertion: "The nation that reverences God will be blessed by God. The nation that rejects God will be rejected by God. The choice is ours. Blessed, blessed is the nation whose God is the Lord."[64]

On the surface, these statements may seem innocent enough. However, the underlying assumptions are quite problematic. Can, for instance, the United States secure God's blessings through moral action or by being a nation that "reverences God" (whatever that might mean)? If we continue to live according to the "spirit of the Christian religion" (again, whatever that might mean), should we really believe that "no great harm can come to our country"? While we are right to concern ourselves with morality to the extent that we are also concerned with matters of social justice, Christians must recognize that morality cannot secure God's blessing because to be a "nation whose God is the Lord" demands not a general adherence to biblical principles or the Judeo-Christian ethic, but a commitment to Christ.[65]

Even if Christians could convince (though not convert) the populous and influence politicians so that the United States returned to something approximating the Judeo-Christian ethic, it isn't clear that doing so would mean that the United States would become a "nation whose God is the Lord."[66] Worse, if Christians make efforts to convince and influence rather than testify and convert, we will likely begin to focus on specific moral issues rather than on discipleship. In doing so, we open up a range of means for moral compliance that doesn't necessarily require the proclamation of the gospel. To what extent can the body of Christ be a faithful presence in the world if our primary objective becomes adherence to a select set of moral issues rather than pointing the lost to Christ? As we hold on to what once "was," we run the risk of distorting God and what it means to follow Him. We run the risk of shifting our loyalties away from God and toward a semi-utopian vision that only loosely incorporates God.

That semi-utopian vision is problematic because it frames our understanding of reality. If we believe, as Jeffress asserts in his sermon, that there is a necessity to preserve the Christian heritage of the United States, we will likely engage in activities that are intended to preserve that heritage *and believe that engaging in such activities is right*. In doing so, we pursue that end

~ 43 ~

not through any means necessary but with the assumption that the means we use to accomplish that end complement or fit within the stream of God's activity of making all things new. Instead of focusing our efforts on being a people whose lives are dedicated to proclaiming "the excellencies of him who called you out of darkness into his marvelous light," we can become a people whose passion to see morality instituted in a broken world becomes more important than God. To put it differently, if the preservation of America's Christian heritage (whatever it might be) becomes our goal, it is difficult to believe that we will be able to be "all things to all people" (1 Cor 9:22).

Paul's argument in 1 Corinthians 9 is, to some degree, against preservation and heritage. Paul was a Jew, yet, having encountered Jesus on the road to Damascus, he is not interested in the preservation of Judaism as such any more than he is interested in preserving the identity of the Gentiles as such. In becoming "all things to all people," Paul has little concern for generic moral frameworks or the continuation of Jewish or Gentile ethnic and religious identities.[67] Instead, he becomes "all things to all people that by all means I might save some" (1 Cor 9:22). The focus is not on preservation but on salvation.

One question with which Christians in the United States must wrestle involves how participation within the apparatus of a representative democracy allows and/or precludes us from following Paul's example of being "all things to all people." Has our desire to return to a more morally comfortable context overshadowed our desire to see the lost transformed into the image of Christ "by grace through faith" (Eph 2:8–9)? It is not so much that moral issues should not concern Christians. At the propositional level, Christians are to ensure they are not calling "evil good and good evil" (Isa 5:20). We know *that* certain actions are evil. My concern is not so much with what we affirm as with *how* we affirm.

We may lament the loss of a moral environment in which Christians shared certain norms of behavior with non-Christians; however, it isn't always clear why we lament such a loss. Many people who were basically moral in the eyes of other humans continue to refuse to acknowledge Christ. To put it differently, a so-called "Christian nation" is not genuinely

Christian unless Christ is indispensable to what it means to be Christian. Instead, the phrase "Christian nation" seems to refer less to a nation whose "God is the Lord" and more to a nation whose policies and practices have been influenced to some significant (though selective and incomplete) degree by Christians or Christian principles.[68] We should ask ourselves what is truly accomplished by seeking to recapture a "Christian heritage" that is not rooted in Christ.

A desire to preserve institutions, stories, values, or principles that have become nostalgic in the name of Christ is, at best, wrongheaded. Jeffress's assertion that "the nation that reverences God will be blessed by God" gestures toward a subtle falsehood in so much as it connects the preservation of a nation (e.g., the United States) with the continuation of certain norms or structures that align but are not entirely in accord with the scriptures. If we follow a similar logic, we make a mistake analogous to the false prophets in Jeremiah 7. The temple becomes a symbol of God's ongoing blessing, just as some abstract notion of morality does for the United States. As long as the temple was standing, Israel could have the assurance that God was with them and that "no great harm" would come to Israel. As God highlights through Jeremiah, however, God is not tied to the temple. The temple is not a bottle we rub to get three wishes from "God the genie," nor is exercising morality in selective instances without accepting Christ a guarantee of national prosperity and security.[69] God's presence is fearful (or should be) to all who do not accept Jesus as Lord.

It seems to me that preserving our "Christian heritage" may be having a similar effect. As we seek to bring back a world that was differently broken or broken in a manner more to our liking, we do not "seek first the kingdom of God and his righteousness" (Matt 6:33) but our own sense of the way the world should be. It is not so much that the outcome of our efforts would be an unlivable dystopia but that our efforts would be less directed by God than by our own vision of a well-ordered world (no matter how biblically informed it may seem). As such, Christians must be willing to recognize that there is only one unshakable kingdom (Heb 12:28), one investment that has an eternal return (Matt 5:12; Gal 6:8), and one message that all humanity needs to hear (Rom 1:16; 10:14–17). When we do so, we will be far less consumed with a desire to preserve or restore an environment that is differently broken than the one we have now and far more consumed with Christ and the proclamation of His gospel in deed and in truth to a world that needs to hear it.

Reflecting on Preservation

Scripture Reading

- Isaiah 5:8-30
- Jeremiah 7:1-15
- 1 Corinthians 9:1-23
- Ephesians 2:1-10
- Hebrews 12:18-29

Questions

- Setting aside the practical, day-to-day way of life that I enjoy as a citizen of the United States, what would change in theological perspective if Christianity were to be further marginalized within the United States?
- What am I unwilling to let go of in my life?
- When I consider my interactions with others, am I following Paul's example in trying to be all things to all people in order to save some?

Prayer

- Lord, I'm not sure why I want to preserve the way things are or bring back the way things were. Perhaps I crave stability or comfort. Perhaps I am legitimately concerned about the way others are treated. Perhaps I am just being carried along by the crowd. Whatever the reason, I would ask You to keep me from making a fetish of some utopian vision of my own making or of some issue about which I am particularly passionate. I exist to bring glory to You on Your terms by allowing You to demonstrate Your wisdom through me. Align my desires with Yours and give me patience to act with obedience as I participate with You as You make all things new. Amen.

9 Discernment

"...we not only need to exercise discernment with regard to the information we consume, but constraint and wisdom with regard to the information we produce and present."
—James Spencer, Thinking Christian[70]

What you see is *not* all there is. Yet, despite our information-rich world, we often make decisions based on limited evidence. There isn't always time to rethink every decision we make or to gather additional data. Some decisions need to be more or less automatic. For example, while driving a car, we don't want to rethink the process of removing our foot from the gas and pressing the brake to slow down when we see brake lights ahead. We want that action to be fairly intuitive. We are taking in a great deal of information while driving, but the frameworks we've developed for driving a car allow us to process that information without a great deal of effortful thought.

Economist Daniel Kahneman describes our "mental life by the metaphor of two agents, called System 1 and System 2."[71] System 1 is the fast-thinking agent that constructs "a coherent interpretation of what is going on in our world at any instant."[72] This system "operates automatically and quickly, with little or no effort and no sense of voluntary control."[73] While System 1's coherent stories often approximate reality sufficient to allow for reasonable decision making, "the amount and quality of the data on which the story is based are largely irrelevant."[74] **Because System 1 doesn't discriminate based on "the amount and quality" of data, it is susceptible to a number of decision-making biases.**

Unlike System 1, "System 2 allocates attention to the effortful mental activities that demand it, including complex computations. The operations of System 2 are often associated with the subjective experience of agency, choice, and concentration."[75] System 2 serves as a check and corrective to the intuitions of System 1. The problem is that System 2 is often lazy. It doesn't "check" System 1 in every instance. If it seems easier and/or relatively safe to default to the coherent stories we already believe, we will be *less discerning* in accepting information that fits with our coherent story while more quickly dismissing information that disrupts it.

Understanding Systems 1 and 2 helps us understand some of the more fundamental building blocks of Christian discernment. **First**, we need to build a coherent story about the world that is biblically and theologically faithful so that our intuitions are deeply rooted in our experience of God and His revelation. We need the intuition that comes from an ever-deepening understanding of God's Word because we recognize that Word as the final authority for life and faith in our individual and communal actions.

Second, we need to learn when to curb our intuition, engage in deeper theological reflection, and adjust our intuitions as God gives us renewed insight. As essential as our intuition is, we cannot assume that the coherent story on which it is based is complete or completely right. That is not to say that the scriptures are deficient (they are certainly not), but *our knowledge and understanding of them may be*. As we are confronted by surprising circumstances or by God's Word, or both, we must pause to reconsider our understanding of God, others, ourselves, and the world. System 2 provides our own internal prophetic theologian whose task is "to call out false beliefs and false practices and the false ways of imagining the world that fund them."[76]

These two "building blocks" of Christian discernment are interrelated. We need to develop a Christ-like intuition tempered by a willingness to embrace new insights when confronted with complexities that do not fit our coherent stories. As we align ourselves more closely with Christ, our intuition allows for a pattern of life based on our current understanding of Christ and His Word. Yet, that current understanding will often need revision or expansion as we continually submit ourselves to the teachings of the biblical text and/or experience God in new ways. Without Christ-like intuition (System 1) *and* our own internal prophetic theologian (System 2), our discernments will be either too automatic or too slow. As such, part of discernment involves knowing when to trust our intuitions and when to curb them by engaging in deeper biblical and theological reflections that will root out falsehood and correct and reorient our intuitions.

Consider, for instance, the dynamics within the book of Job. Having lost his property, his children, and his health, Job is visited by Eliphaz, Bildad, and Zophar, three friends who "come to show him sympathy and comfort him" (2:11). After sitting with Job in his suffering for seven days (2:13) and listening to Job's initial lament (3:1–26), the friends begin to offer Job counsel about his situation, encouraging him to admit his sin to God so that he might find relief (4:6–11; 8:1–7; 20–22; 11:1–6; 15:1–11; 22:1–11; 21–30). They view all that is happening to Job as a sign that Job has been unfaithful. They can see it no other way because they believe that the wicked perish while the innocent prosper. The friends advocate for the "retribution principle," which "indicates that there is a norm that decides which actions will bring good or bad consequences for the acting person."[77]

While the picture that Job's friends offer is not false *per se*, it does not apply to Job's situation. As biblical scholar Elaine Phillips puts it, Eliphaz, Bildad, and Zophar "erred in consistently slipping Job into their moral formulas," which "constituted 'false testimony' because it ran counter to the public witness to his character."[78] By too quickly defaulting to the coherent story of retributive justice, Job's friends fail to consider that their "blameless and upright" friend, "who feared God and turned away from evil" (Job 1:1), might be experiencing something other than divine retribution. Their error leads them to misrepresent the particular situation they are addressing and to become false witnesses against Job.

Assuming that they understand what is happening also keeps Job's friends from addressing God. Job is not interested in some abstract system of retribution. Instead, he desires to understand his particular situation and to have his relationship with God restored because "Nothing could be more alien to his [Job's] thought, and to Israelite religion in general, than to isolate the relationship with God as the only thing of value for a man, rendering him indifferent to poverty, callous in bereavement, heedless of pain."[79] Job is driven to God not by abstract principles but by the disruption of his settled world and a desire for understanding and restoration.

Unlike Job, his friends have little reason to struggle with Job's suffering on a theological level. What they see makes sense because they assume Job's guilt. They see no contradiction between the way they believe the world works and the state of affairs with which they are not confronted. As such, they default to an abstract framework that has no room for variance: God blesses the righteous and punishes the wicked (4:7–11). By refusing to release their grip on the coherent narrative of the retribution principle, Job's friends miss an opportunity to interact with God and to receive fresh insight.

Like Job's friends, we may be too committed to a particular understanding of God and His Word, which leads us to be less-than discerning. As Anderson observes, "His [Job's] friends talk about God. Job talks to God. And this makes him the only authentic theologian in the book."[80] When we become overly committed to our coherent stories, we risk talking about God rather than to him. We don't wrestle with reality. Prayer becomes something we do after deciding what we will do before coming to God in prayer. It is difficult to identify such a process as "discernment" because we do not discern simply by developing a coherent story about what it means to live by faith but by remaining open to new insights as God moves beyond the limits of such a story.

Our ability to make God-honoring decisions involves what theologian Samuel Wells calls "the time of moral effort," during which people "form skills and habits—habits that mean people take the right things for granted and skills that give them the ability to do the things they take for granted."[81] The notion of taking "the right things for granted" approximates the intuitive operation of System 1, as well as the ability to shift to the more effortful reflection of System 2. As we develop a more coherent understanding of God, ourselves, others, and the world, certain actions will become automatic. Yet, one of the "right things" we must learn to take for granted is the need to engage System 2. We can't simply depend on our intuition because, no matter how coherent our story may be, it remains subject to God's revision.

As such, to be discerning, we need to remain open to new insights, which constitute new patterns for living in God's presence.[82] Remaining open involves challenging our settled understandings by addressing God through prayer and studying His Word. In doing so, we do not set aside the truth or "call evil good and good evil" (Isa 5:20). Instead, we learn to trust our intuition while continually being aware that we are still people in the process. To discern, then, involves (1) recognizing when our understanding has reached its limit so that we are no longer representing God truly (or as truly as we might) and (2) pausing rather than stubbornly barreling forward to allow God to speak so that we might convey Christ more truly in a broken world.

Reflecting on Discernment

Scripture Reading

- Job 1:1-2:10
- Job 4:1-5:27
- Job 8:1-22
- Job 11:1-20
- Job 21:1-34

Questions

- How am I holding God at arm's length by leaning on *my understanding* of who He is rather than addressing Him so that He can expand my understanding of who He is?
- How much time do I really take to discern versus simply trusting my intuitions about God, His Word, and what it means to be a Christian in today's world?
- In what ways do I jump to conclusions when I see others in pain or interact with those who may hold a different position than I do in matters of politics or religion?

Prayer

- God, life often seems too clear to me. In part, I know that is because You have enlightened me by giving me eyes to see and ears to hear. Yet, I know that even clarity can be deceptive. Help me to develop the discernment to know when my knowledge and understanding have reached their limits. Keep me from assuming that I understand You so well that I no longer need to struggle with You in prayer. Give me the sensitivity to trust all You have taught me while recognizing that I have much more to learn. Amen.

10 Effort

"Christians will leave the world broken, perhaps more broken despite our faithful efforts to live out the kingdom of God within it. We do not faithfully convey God to the world by fixing the world. We convey Him to the world by continuing to be faithful as we confront a world so broken only God can fix it."
—James Spencer, *Thinking Christian*[83]

What if our efforts have actually been hindering our discipleship? We often think of effort as some intentional exertion, but effort often results in habit so that a "choice that once required effort is now automatic."[84] Efforts that were once deliberate may become unthinking habits. A misdirected or undisciplined effort may prepare us to live in ways that do *not* reflect Christ. Our efforts, even those that seem right and legitimate, will likely result in negative consequences. We can't always anticipate what our efforts will bring, either individually or collectively.

Philosopher Nick Bostrom, for instance, has proposed "the vulnerable world hypothesis" (VWH), suggesting that, "If technological development continues then a set of capabilities will at some point be attained that make the devastation of civilization extremely likely, unless civilization sufficiently exits the semi-anarchic default condition."[85] The semi-anarchic condition, according to Bostrom, consists of our limited capacities for preventive policing and global governance, as well as the diverse motivations of those who develop and/or use new technologies.[86]

These new technologies are not limited to "machines and physical devices," but include "other kinds of instrumentally efficacious templates and procedures" such as "scientific ideas, institutional designs, organizational techniques, ideologies, concepts, and memes."[87] Bostrom rightly recognizes that our technologies are dangerous because we are unaware of how the technologies we create will benefit or disadvantage humanity. Our world is vulnerable to human efforts *that are unguided and unrestrained by God and His Word*. Like a baby's mobile, we can't fully anticipate how touching one side will make the rest of the mobile move. We can only anticipate that it will. As we exercise our God-given capacities without the guidance and restraints of God, we seek to fix the world in ways that seem right in our own eyes.

Bostrom's hypothesis gestures toward our seemingly limitless capacity to engage in unrestrained and unguided efforts as we seek to navigate the world's brokenness in the most comfortable way possible. Like the tower builders at Babel, we identify a problem we all share (11:4), coordinate together to solve that problem (11:1), consider the technologies available to us (11:3), and set out to establish an identity for ourselves in the world (11:4). The tower builders were ignorant of God and what He desired. Their coordination, ambition, and technological capacity allowed them to pursue a goal that would have solidified (or at least extended) their self-sufficiency. God Himself recognizes, "Behold, they are one people, and they have all one language, and this is only the beginning of what they will do. And nothing that they propose to do will now be impossible for them" (11:6).

Our efforts can fool us into thinking that the world is making progress because of improving trends in various areas.[88] While we should celebrate improvements to the human condition where we can find them, we should be wary of thinking that human technologies have caused or can guarantee or even sustain such so-called progress (cf. Deut 8:17). In part, we should be wary because progress assumes that we understand with sufficient clarity the desired state toward which we are moving from our current state. Yet, outside of Christian eschatology, human hopes and dreams are misdirected, and thus, what we identify as progress is often accompanied by some form of deterioration.[89]

Despite an unclear vision of the desired state toward which we should be moving, our ideologies, institutional designs, and organizational techniques define the "good" and the measures used to assess progress toward that good. Human efforts that contribute to the improvement of those measures are deemed efficient and beneficial. Certain efforts are recognized as having utility because they lead toward the good or even the *greater good*.[90] Others' efforts may be seen as neutral under certain conditions, while others are viewed as hindering the good and are prohibited or discouraged in a variety of ways. It is tempting to accept these human notions of "good" and the associated idea of "progress," yet "good" and "progress" are often achieved in ways that point us and others away from God rather than toward Him. In such cases, **we should consider whether our efforts reflect a shift in our allegiance from God to the good**.

As Christians, we do not believe we can fix the world. The Bible does not suggest that God's people are the solution to brokenness, but rather an embodied demonstration of God's redemption and renewed creative work. Not being able to fix the world does not mean we become callous to those who are hurting. It doesn't mean that we remain silent and passive as others dishonor God. It means that our efforts are directed toward being and making disciples even when the world's technologies seem to offer a more pragmatic path toward progress. We are to use "unrighteous mammon" to "make friends" who will receive us into eternal dwellings when that unrighteous mammon fails (Lk 16:9), but our efforts are not guided by the logic of unrighteous mammon or the world's technologies. They are guided by a recognition that both will fail.

What might effort aimed at discipleship involve? In part, it involves something akin to what Nietzsche described as "learning to see," by which he meant overcoming "the inability to resist a stimulus—you *must* react, you follow every impulse."[91] To learn to see in this manner requires us to develop the discipline sufficient to keep our bodies "under control" so that we are not "disqualified" for having preached to others (1 Cor 9:27). The "self-control" of the athlete is comparable to the self-control to be exercised in the Christian life. Such discipline is aimed at avoiding the mistakes of Israel and the judgment some of the Israelites suffered (10:1–

22). As we run so as to obtain the prize, we do so with self-control and intentionality rather than "as one beating the air" (9:24–26).

We do not exert "moral effort" in the sense that we muster our own strength to follow Jesus. Instead, our effort is, to a large extent, a matter of disrupting the habits and patterns of a broken world. Yet, this disruption is not achieved by our own willpower because even our most noble "human precepts and teachings... are of no value in stopping the indulgence of the flesh" (Col 2:23). We disrupt the fallen world's patterns by following God's path. The effort, then, is a matter of re-patterning our lives as we learn "the secret of the easy yoke," which involves "the intelligent, informed, unyielding resolve to live as Jesus lived in all aspects of his life, not just in the moment of specific choice or action."[92]

Our efforts are devoted to developing a rhythm and cadence of life patterned on God's wisdom. There is a sense, then, in which our effort is directed toward prioritizing God because, for Christians, "discipline is the human effort to unveil what has been covered, to bring to the foreground what has remained hidden, and to put on the lamp stand what has been kept under a basket."[93]

It is "the effort to avoid deafness and to become sensitive to the sound of the voice that calls us by a new name and invites us to a new life of discipleship."[94] As such, our efforts are not aimed toward self-improvement or the improvement of the world, but toward a reprioritization reflected by and in our patterns of life. We orient the whole of our lives around God, allowing His wisdom to guide us and His never-ending lovingkindness to cultivate a trust in us that prompts us to obey even when obedience does not make sense.

Reflecting on Effort

Scripture Reading

- Genesis 11:1-9
- Romans 12:1-8
- 1 Corinthians 9:1-27
- 1 Corinthians 10:1-22
- Colossians 2:16-23

Questions

- To what degree am I patterning my life according to the "technologies" of this world rather than taking up the "easy yoke" of Christ?
- How have I become like the tower builders of Babel by relying on my own capacities, following my own judgement and rationality, and seeking to establish an identity for myself apart from God?
- How do I demonstrate my commitment to discipleship and my trust in God through the rhythms of my life?

Prayer

- Lord, I put in effort for many things. I push myself to excel in my career, to care for my family, and to build a reputation for myself. I even put effort into studying Your Word and seeking to grow in my faith. However good my intentions may be, if I am honest, I am often trying to pursue my own agendas and address my own concerns. I am often ready for You to change me in the ways I desire to be changed, rather than being radically open to Your transformation. I don't always want the easy yoke of Christ because the weight of my own effort gives me a sense of substance and worth. Yet, I am to find my worth in You.
- Please transform my efforts so that they are no longer my vain attempts at self-improvement but an ongoing effort to remain awake and alert that I may see You more clearly and trust You more deeply. Amen.

11 Testimony

"If we take seriously biblical statements about speech and the tongue, about the nature of pure religion, and about truth and love within the community of faith, I believe we will find it difficult to justify the sort of public testimony to which we seem to have become accustomed."
—James Spencer, *Thinking Christian*[95]

In February 1974, Alexander Solzhenitsyn was stripped of his Soviet citizenship and deported to Frankfurt, West Germany. On the same day, he released an essay titled "Live Not by Lies."[96] In the essay, Solzhenitsyn offers an analysis of totalitarian regimes and those who live in them noting,

> "We hope only not to stray from the herd, not to set out on our own, and risk suddenly having to make do without the white bread, the hot water heater, a Moscow residency permit. We have internalized well the lessons drummed into us by the state; we are forever content and comfortable with its premise: we cannot escape the environment, the social conditions; they shape us, "being determines consciousness." What have we to do with this? We can do nothing. But we can do— everything!—even if we comfort and lie to ourselves that this is not so. It is not "they" who are guilty of everything, but we ourselves, only we!."[97]

Having spent eight years in a Russian labor camp, Solzhenitsyn is not speaking as someone unfamiliar with the consequences of dissension. Yet, he urges those living under totalitarianism *not to assist* the regime in propagating lies.

Solzhenitsyn notes that those living under totalitarianism must choose whether to "remain a witting servant of the lies (needless to say, not due to natural predisposition, but in order to provide a living for the family, to rear the children in the spirit of lies!)" or to shrug off the lies "to stand as an honest man, worthy of the respect of his children and contemporaries."[98] He goes on to offer seven refusals that illustrate a "personal nonparticipation in lies." These refusals preclude:

- the propagation of falsehood through written, verbal, artistic means,
- participation in meetings, rallies, or other such events that are structured to advance a specific ideological viewpoint
- voting for proposals one does not support or candidates deemed "dubious or unworthy,"[99]
- continued interaction with speakers who "utter a lie, ideological drivel, or shameless propaganda" or "a newspaper or journal that distorts or hides the underlying facts."[100]

For Solzhenitsyn, these refusals represent a negative testimony in which we must "at least refuse to say what we do not think."[101]

As Christians, particularly Christians in the United States, we don't live under a totalitarian regime. Yet, we are often subject to seemingly inevitable and irresistible forces that are "like parasites, they can only survive when attached to a person."[102] Like those whom Solzhenitsyn addresses in "Live Not by Lies," we are often comfortable being a particular sort of dishonest. As our digital age has made it easier to publish and consume information, we've become comfortable, for instance, spreading subtle falsehoods couched in political statements, personal agendas, or common ways of speaking. We have resigned ourselves to voting for one of two or perhaps three candidates, whether or not we believe any of those candidates is worthy of representing us. We continue to consume and share content in ways that put us at a higher risk of acquiring or propagating false beliefs. In many ways, it would seem, Christians need to learn to live not by lies if we are to offer faithful testimony to the God we serve.

It is tempting to think that our testimony is a matter of truth-telling only. If we speak the truth and do good deeds, our testimony to Christ is faithful. Yet, as we find throughout the scriptures, God urges us to avoid spreading a false report (Exod 23:1), walking in the way of sinners (Ps 1:1; Prov 1:8–19), spreading strife (Prov 16:28), praying like hypocrites and Gentiles (Matt 6:5-8), or speaking evil about others (Tit 3:2). Our testimony is not as faithful as it could be if we are loving "in word or talk" rather than "in deed and in truth" (1 Jn 3:18).

Our testimony is faithful in the sense that our "words and deed… stand to the 'realities' they [we] believe in, rather as reports stand to the realities they are about."[103] Testifying to the truth involves more than making assertions about right and wrong. It involves our posture and demeanor. How we deliver a message is crucial because we are not attempting to argue a proposition so much as we are seeking to demonstrate the reality of God and all that means for a broken world. Our testimony is "about making things real" so that God, who is real, becomes "salient."[104] Testifying may involve activities such as asserting, debating, rebuking, and educating. Yet, these activities should not distract from God. We are not in the business of drawing the eyes of others away from Christ but *toward Him* through our testimony.

In the Sermon on the Mount, Jesus describes "behavior or attitudes that are characteristic of the group" that will inherit the Kingdom.[105] Those who mourn, hunger and thirst for righteousness, make peace, are poor in spirit, meek, merciful, and pure in heart (5:4–8), demonstrate themselves to be part of the community of Christ. Those who would join themselves to Jesus are not persecutors or revilers. Instead, they are persecuted and reviled (5:11–12). The testimony of those who were part of Christ's community was conveyed through their distinctive way of life, which constituted "not… in some ethical principle, but in the very person of Jesus Christ."[106]

As Christians, we testify to Christ regardless of our own agendas and desires or the potential negative consequences that may come as a result of such testimony. Testifying to Christ may not appear particularly expedient. Often, it can seem like a wasted effort when considered pragmatically. Like Jeremiah, we may find ourselves weary of offering testimony yet incapable of remaining silent (Jer 20:8–9). However, expediency and pragmatism are often the enemies of faithful testimony.

We are not in the business of directing attention to ourselves or even to issues of legitimate concern. We do not want people to "seek merely the catchiness of the idea, the person, or the prospect, and not the substance of its consequence or the reservoir of its competence."[107] "Catchiness" may well be more effective in the near term, but our goal is to be faithful in planting and watering even if God never produces the growth for which we hope (1 Cor 3:6). Faithfulness, in other words, is our primary target. Effectiveness may follow, but it cannot become the end that justifies any means.

Learning to live not by lies will require Christians to develop a more radical commitment to the truth. Such a commitment will not safeguard us against mistakes. Instead, it will remind us why confession is a sign of our membership in the body of Christ (1 Jn 1:9). Our confession of sin is a crucial part of the testimony we offer because, through confession, we demonstrate our conviction that being truthful is more important than appearing perfect. In confession, we count whatever shame we may feel or negative consequences we may experience from revealing our sin as less important than living in the light of the truth.

As we develop a more radical commitment to the truth, we will not only find confession more natural but also the proclamation of the gospel. We will come to see beyond the terribly simple notions proposed by those "capable of providing some semblance of a solution or promising a world free of at least some of our frustrations."[108] Perhaps more importantly, we will avoid becoming "demagogues who seek power by exploiting the ire and frustration of the population and making appealing, but 'terribly simplified' and, ultimately, deceitful promises."[109] To be radically committed to the truth is to learn to "seek, speak, and show understanding of what God was doing in Christ for the sake of the world."[110]

The goal of our testimony is not to draw people by any means but to offer an honest account of the God we serve through our words and deeds. As we consider what it means to be truly honest, we must recognize that our participation in divisive or degrading speech, our endorsement of that which is unworthy of God, or our unwillingness to admit that prioritizing the various ways the world is broken may well lead us away from impartiality and toward dishonesty. To offer a faithful testimony, we must keep to God and His commission for us to be and make disciples in the foreground, because when our testimony ceases to be about all God has done in Christ, we can be sure we have more to learn about living not by.

Reflecting on Testimony

Scripture Reading

- Exodus 23:1-9
- Proverbs 1:8-19
- Jeremiah 20:1-18
- Matthew 5:1-12
- 1 Corinthians 3:1-23

Questions

- How have I aligned myself with lies?
- To what extent am I participating in conversations that are divisive and polarizing rather than pointing others to Christ?
- If I had to assess where my testimony about Christ falls apart, where would it be? Am I prepared to confess my mistakes and failures and to renew my commitment to being truly honest?

Prayer

- Lord, in asking us to be and make disciples, You also give us the task of reflecting You in the world. We are salt and light. We are Your people who are to demonstrate Your manifold wisdom in the world. Help me to offer a faithful testimony to You. Show me when I am pushing You to the background and privileging a position, person, or purpose above pointing others to You. Guide me that, as I seek to care for those who are being treated unjustly or who are experiencing brokenness in some specific way, I may do so in deed and in truth. Help me not to become so consumed with fixing the world that I forget to be faithful to You. Amen.

12 Inclusion

"If we continually have our own perceptions, urges, instincts, preferences, or 'expertise' (what we currently 'know' about the world or a particular topic) reinforced through the narrowing of the amount of information we are able to access, we run the risk of becoming entrenched and dismissive of opposing views of the world."
—James Spencer, *Thinking Christian*[111]

When Jesus says he has come to fulfill Isaiah 61:1-2, those listening to his teaching in the synagogue initially "spoke well of him and marveled at the gracious words that were coming from his mouth" (Lk 4:22). Yet, as Jesus continues speaking, He tells the stories of Elijah and Zarephath, the widow from the land of Sidon, and of Elisha and Naaman the Syrian (Lk 4:25–27). The implication of Jesus' teaching was clear enough: the good news would be proclaimed to the Gentiles. The people quickly turn on Jesus and seek to "throw him down the cliff" (Lk 4:29).

Throughout his ministry, Jesus includes outcasts despite the objections raised by the Pharisees, who believe Jesus is violating Mosaic law by healing those on the margins of society. The Pharisees and teachers of the law objected to many of Jesus' ministry practices because they ignored the forgiveness and healing that marked Jesus as "the one who is to come" (Lk 7:20) because of their focus on the religious regulations they identified with the Mosaic law. In the minds of the Pharisees, Jesus is diminishing the religious regulations that have preserved Jewish identity in Rome by forgiving sins (Lk 5:17–26), eating with tax collectors and sinners (5:27–32), healing on the Sabbath (6:6–11), and inspiring a ragtag group of disciples who do not fast (5:33–39) or honor the Sabbath (6:1–5).

Jesus did not eat with tax collectors and sinners because he believed them to be pious. He was not authorizing their lifestyles. He ate with them because "Those who are well have no need of a physician, but those who are sick. I have not come to call the righteous but sinners to repentance" (Lk 5:31–32). Jesus sees no need to exclude those who have been excluded.

The Pharisees, however, see things differently. In their minds, Jesus is not ushering in the kingdom of God but misleading the people by encouraging them to diminish, if not disobey, the law and to break with the systems they have put in place to define Judaism. In claiming to be the Christ while transgressing the boundaries set by the religious leaders, Jesus, in the mind of the Pharisees, is not the long-awaited Messiah. Offering sight to the blind, hearing to the deaf, release to the captives, and liberty to the oppressed may have been fine had Jesus done it according to the rules established by the Pharisees. The Pharisees, in some sense, excluded themselves from Jesus' ministry.

By keeping sinners, tax collectors, and the ritually unclean at arm's length, the Pharisees have already closed themselves off to the adjacent possibilities that life with such individuals could produce. At the very least, keeping company with those who have been discarded by the rest of society offers the potential to benefit from the unexpected gifts the discarded may bring. Moreover, doing for the "least of these" becomes the mark of a community that knows Jesus (Matt 25:31–46). The Pharisees are locked into their established paradigm. Their closed theoretical framework blinds them to the adjacent possibilities around them. Having closed themselves off from the marginalized, they also close themselves off from Jesus.

While Jesus includes outcasts in his ministry, He does so to call them to repentance (Lk 5:32). Salvation was not without implications in so much as it involved following Jesus and observing his commands. Inclusion was not a matter of releasing people into an "anything goes" lifestyle but of alerting them to "the year of the Lord's favor" (Isaiah 61:2; Lk 4:19) and the necessity of repentance (Lk 24:27). One could be included in the ministry of Jesus and still be excluded from the kingdom of God. Rejecting Jesus meant rejecting the life of the kingdom that He provided.

When we hear the term "inclusion" in today's world, it is often in combination with "diversity" and "equity." This combination of words can be used to demand that all lifestyles, characteristics, or choices be deemed legitimate. They can also be used to combat the prejudices and partialities that often create new classes of vulnerable, marginalized outcasts in today's world. While diversity, equity, and inclusion programs have a myriad of problems, one glaring difficulty lies in the *telos* or final aim, of such programs. If, for instance, inclusion is confused with acceptance, we will likely lose the ability to call others to repentance with regard to certain behaviors. Jesus recognizes the diverse audiences to whom he speaks as equally in need of being included in the message of salvation, which should prompt repentance and would require discipleship.

As Christians, both individually and collectively, we need to take care not to exclude any group from the message of salvation. When we withhold from one group or another the message of salvation and the repentance it requires, we tend to exhibit certain theological mistakes. **First**, consider Jonah's refusal to preach repentance to Nineveh. His hatred for the Ninevites drives him to disobey God. Jonah does not only see the Ninevites as an irredeemably lost cause but as unworthy of the salvation God has asked him to present to them. Jonah did not want the Ninevites to be saved (Jon 4:3–4). His mistake was not in his characterization of God as "gracious... and merciful, slow to anger and abounding in steadfast love, and relenting from disaster" (4:2). It was because of his unwillingness to accept that God would show such grace to the people of Nineveh. Perhaps we should ask ourselves whether we have become too much like Jonah in our dealings with those we have identified as our opposition.

Second, if we are willing to write off "tax collectors and sinners" as irredeemable, we place constraints on the God who has no constraints. This mistake is closer to that made by the Pharisees, who were blind to the possibility that God was not limited by their systems or traditions. Jesus' ministry demonstrated that God was living and active beyond the boundaries constructed by the religious leaders of the day. We see a similar dynamic in the stoning of Stephen in Acts 7. Having been accused of speaking against the temple and Moses (Acts 6:11–14), Stephen responds by narrating the numerous times when God worked beyond the confines of the temple or the nation of Israel (7:2-53). God does not work within limits. When we exclude others from the message of salvation, we may be placing an artificial constraint on God and underestimating the power of the gospel.

Finally, we can assume that calling others to repentance is a form of *exclusion*. As such, we draw individuals toward a Jesus whose expectations and values align suspiciously with our own. This method of withholding the message of salvation instills inclusion with a strong dose of individualism and human-centeredness so that one's life is determined less by Christ and more by one's own thoughts and feelings, as well as the thoughts and feelings of the community of which one is a part. It may seem odd to think of inclusion as a means of exclusion, yet inclusion in a community willing to call "evil good and good evil" (Isa 5:20) is not an inclusion in the message of salvation. It is a *de facto* exclusion because it denies the transformative decision that the gospel requires. When we accept Christ, we are not only saved from death but also from the fallen state that caused it.

Jesus did not offer outcasts inclusion into the kingdom on their own terms, yet he was not afraid to *include himself* with outcasts to proclaim to them the way of salvation. As we seek to be inclusive, we should keep in mind that we are not including people in the kingdom but in the message of salvation. That message leaves *no one* who accepts it unchanged, nor is it a message that requires one to change before receiving it. When we orient ourselves toward inclusion, we do not embrace the notion that God has no moral standards but that all are invited to consider the gospel. Inclusion welcomes everyone to conform to the image of Jesus Christ.

Reflecting on Inclusion

Scripture Reading

- Jonah 1-4
- Luke 4:16-30
- Luke 5:17-6:11
- Luke 7:18-35
- Acts 6:8-7:60

Questions

- Who are the people in your life that you are excluding from the message of salvation? Why?
- To what extent have you built walls that constrain God?
- How do we, as Christians, exclude others from the message of salvation?

Prayer

- God, we recognize that we are not more deserving of your salvation than anyone else. We do not want to be like Jonah or the Pharisees, who opposed your kingdom in their own ways. Help us to include everyone in the message of salvation. Help us to proclaim your gospels to others, even when we don't believe they will change. Amen.

13 Accountability

"We need not resign ourselves to live in a world without hope for imminent change and ultimate transformation."
—James Spencer, Thinking Christian[112]

In a lecture titled "Maybe We Just Need a Different Chicken... Politeness and Civility in the Function of Contemporary Ideology," philosopher and cultural critic Slavoj Žižek suggests that the influence of ideology goes deeper than we often recognize. It is embedded in the way we see the world and the questions we ask about it. According to Žižek:

> "Ideology is efficient because it deals with very real problems... ecology, racism, and so on. The lesson is that there are not only wrong answers to questions. There are also wrong questions in the sense that the very way we perceive a problem, which can be a very real problem, is effectively a part of the problem."[113]

Ideologies are not necessarily wrong, but they *are always incomplete*.[114] As such, the questions ideologies prompt us to ask and the solutions they suggest will never fully account for all that is going on in the world.

By "imposing a pattern—some form of structure or organization—on how we read (and misread) political fact, events, occurrences, actions, on how we see images and hear voices," ideologies help us to make sense of the world in at least two ways.[115] **First**, they allow us to "shape" reality. Shaping reality doesn't refer to bending what we would normally consider "objective reality." It doesn't refer to certain postmodern notions of relativity. Instead, this shaping changes the way we participate with reality as we recognize (if only partially) what our environment offers us and ascribe symbolic meaning to it. Our recognition of what a certain portion of reality provides or "means" does not change reality as such because "an affordance is not bestowed upon an object by a need of an observer and his act of perceiving it" but "the object offers what it does because it is what it is."[116]

To understand this shaping function, consider the difference between taking a bath and being baptized. In the former instance, there is a human body and water in a space large enough for immersion. In a religious ceremony, the same elements are transformed in the context of a broader ritual. They take on a new symbolic significance. Through a combination of additional words and actions, water becomes more than a vehicle for cleanliness. It becomes a symbolic medium used to represent, among other things, a burial (Rom 6:4). Water not only affords us the ability to meet more mundane needs, such as avoiding dehydration or removing dirt from the body, but also conveys a tangible act of surrender that has taken place through faith.

Second, ideologies provide a sense of stability and order. By imposing a pattern, ideologies create practical stability. This stability has practical usefulness but is often sustained by fantasy. When an ideology reaches its limit, those who hold it have a few options. First, they can admit those limits and continue to hold to the ideology for its practical effects. Second, they can modify the ideology so that it aligns more closely with reality. Finally, they create a story (a fantasy) that will allow the ideology to continue to operate despite seeming contradictions.

Think, for example, of meritocracy or the notion that people are selected based on their ability. As an ideological idea, we may agree that people should be selected for roles based on their ability to perform those roles. However, asserting that we live in a meritocracy requires a fantasy. How, for instance, do those who inherit intergenerational wealth fit into meritocracies? While a previous generation may have had the talent and ability to make a fortune, there is no guarantee that the next generation has the same sort of savvy. Would the next generation have merited wealth and success had they not had a leg up from their more talented parents? The point is not to move toward some equally fantastic socialist fantasy or to claim privilege whenever anyone has some advantage. Instead, it is simply to highlight the fact that ideologies exhibit broad sense-making patterns that, when taken too far, ignore or squeeze out aspects of reality that don't fit with the ideology.

So, how does all of this talk of ideology relate to accountability? **First**, while we should certainly think about accountability in terms of personal holiness and moral formation, ideology points to a broader sense in which we must hold one another accountable. If we are capable of both shaping reality and defaulting to the comfort of the status quo in ways that skew or deny the reality of God, we must concern ourselves with more than "bad acts." We must also concern ourselves with holding one another accountable for (1) participating in reality by recognizing all God has afforded and ascribing to reality meanings governed by God's Word and (2) *not* accepting ideological notions as more complete than they actually are so that we begin to fit God, ourselves, others, and creation into an incomplete ideological pattern.

Writing to the church in Colossae, Paul identifies the dangers of being taken "captive by philosophy and empty deceit, according to human tradition, according to elemental spirits of the world, and not according to Christ" (Col 2:8). He tells them to "let no one pass judgment on you in questions of food and drink, or with regard to a festival or a new moon or a Sabbath" (2:16). Paul's exhortation involves a caution against trading a pattern of sense-making that is according to Christ for one that is "not according to Christ." In other words, he is cautioning the church in Colossae against navigating life via an incomplete and ultimately incorrect ideological map that would cause them to "submit to regulations— 'Do not handle, Do not taste, Do not touch'—according to human precepts and teachings" (Col 2:20-21).

The danger Paul warns against is one that would change the way the Colossians participate in the world. He does not want them to ascribe meanings to "food and drink, or with regard to a festival or a new moon or a Sabbath" that would hinder their walk with Christ because "the substance belongs to Christ" (Col 2:16–17). By defaulting to the status quo, which others seek to impose on them and the world, the Colossians run the risk of engaging in practices with "an appearance of wisdom" that "are of no value in stopping the indulgence of the flesh" (2:23).

If we consider ideology to be a form of "philosophy and empty deceit, according to human tradition, according to the elemental spirits" (Col 2:8), we recognize the need for accountability that reaches beyond immoral action. We need to practice accountability that analyzes the patterns by which other members of the body of Christ and we live. As with the church in Colossae, **we will often find ourselves tempted to live according to the patterns of our ideological maps rather than allowing God to chart a theological course for us**. Like those who use physical maps, we "willingly tolerate white lies on maps" and make it easier for ideological cartographers "to also tell more serious lies."[117]

What we need to recover through accountability (and a variety of other mechanisms) is a commitment to discipleship. To do so requires that we hold one another accountable for (a) adopting patterns of life that demonstrate our belief in Christ and (b) rejecting patterns that promote falsehood. This sort of accountability might be applied, for instance, to the way we engage in conversations about social issues in the public square. If our passion for an issue causes us to diminish those who hold a different viewpoint or to neglect those impacted by an issue, we are unlikely to be living in alignment with Christ's ministry (Matt 9:9–13; Lk 15:1–32) or our own commission and calling (Matt 28:20; Jam 1:27).[118]

While we are often right to take up the charge against certain ideologies, we are wrong to do so as if we are citizens of the world rather than citizens of Heaven (Phil 3:20). Our approach matters. **If we have adopted ideologies that frame the way we "perceive real problems" apart from Christ, it is likely that we will pursue solutions that do not point to Christ**. We must hold one another accountable to move and see theologically, not ideologically, so that God's people can see the problems of the day with theological eyes, address those problems as those who know the God who redeems sinners, and take seriously the commission to go and make disciples of Christ.

Reflecting on Accountability

Scripture Reading

- Matthew 9:9-13
- Luke 15:1-32
- Philippians 3:12-21
- Colossians 2:6-23
- James 1:27

Questions

- How do I usually describe the problems the world faces? How are my descriptions of those problems lacking? Am I too focused on solving the problem or winning the fight that I am missing opportunities to point others to Christ?
- What are some of the ways that I'm adopting the "maps" and "patterns" of the world so that I'm acting more in line with some ideology than with Christ?
- What might it look like for me to find others to hold me accountable to more than just avoiding immoral acts? What might it look like for me to hold others accountable? Does the body of Christ even have the space where we could have conversations that would help me, and others sort through some of these matters? What might that space look like?

Prayer

- God, there is much in this world that opposes You. Much of that opposition is evident, yet much of it also tends to be hidden. The subtle lies we accept and the patterns of life we adopt keep us held captive to the philosophies and empty deceit of human traditions and elemental spirits. Please, Lord, provide opportunities for discipleship and accountability that will help me, and the rest of Your people be salt and light in the world. Help us to be strange in ways that point to You. Help us be strange because we are striving to walk in obedience and to reflect Your Son in a broken world. Amen.

14 Conclusion

"Our individual Christian practice may, and perhaps in many cases should, oppose institutions that 'act back' on us as individual image-bearers and as members of the unified body of Christ."
—James Spencer, Thinking Christian[119]

B eing a disciple and making disciples is not an easy task. In many respects, the church has been outcoordinated by the world in the sense that the "common knowledge" of what it means to be and make disciples has been overshadowed by the "common knowledge" of what it means to be a "good" woman, man, wife, husband, child, employee, boss, or friend. At times, we seem to have become "social artifacts" who "carry the culture that is sustained by wise laws and traditions of civility" through "statecraft," which "is, inevitably, soulcraft."[120] Yet, we are not products of the state or our broader society. We are a people set free to learn to observe all Christ has commanded and teach others the same (Matt 28:20; Rom 6:5–14; Gal 5:1–15).

As we learn and teach God's instructions, we will begin to operate against the grain of the world. Opposition is not our goal, but as we live as women and men free from sin, it will become obvious that we no longer conform to the world but increasingly conform to the image of Christ. This resistance is not militant. In fact, part of our resistance is the recognition that forced adherence is ultimately unproductive. As such, we resist the urge to accept morality when what we desire is salvation. The state is to maintain order by disciplining "bad conduct" (Rom 13:1–7). While Christians in a representative democracy have the right to participate in the political realm, we must remember that our primary identity is found "in Christ" and not "in America." As such, we cannot settle for wholesomeness when only holiness will do.

Christians must do all this in the midst of a world that is increasingly proficient at denying and distorting God. The frequency with which we receive information and the urgency with which it is presented can trick us into thinking that what is being said is worthy of our attention. Often, it is not. Yet, the glowing rectangles we carry around with us tend to keep the trivialities of life in the foreground while pushing God to the margins. He does not belong there. He *never* belonged there.

Resisting the world may well involve arguments and debates. I would not deny the appropriateness of engaging in conversation with those who do not believe in Christ (Acts 17:22–34). I would, however, propose that we do not simply proclaim Christ through rational argument. "Being right" is slightly different than conveying Christ rightly. To do the latter also involves something like the advice Paul offers to Timothy: "Have nothing to do with foolish, ignorant controversies; you know that they breed quarrels. And the Lord's servant must not be quarrelsome but kind to everyone, able to teach, patiently enduring evil, correcting his opponents with gentleness" (2 Tim 2:23–25). To convey Christ rightly is to "make a defense to anyone who asks you for a reason for the hope that is in you; yet do it with gentleness and respect, having a good conscience, so that, when you are slandered, those who revile your good behavior in Christ may be put to shame" (1 Pt 3:15–16). We are not simply to "be right," but to convey Christ rightly.

As such, we must take the time to consider how we are being conformed to the world rather than to the image of Christ. Our whole lives proclaim Christ. As such, we resist the urge to assume we know where God would have us go and what God would have us do. Instead, we arrange our lives so that we intentionally listen and look for God rather than hoping to find Him as we rush into the fray. In doing so, we seek to echo the words of John the Baptist: "He [Christ] must increase, but I must decrease" (Jn 3:30). Such is the nature of our resistance. We do not seek to elevate ourselves or solve the world's problems. We seek to position ourselves for

God's use, having been buried with Him through baptism and learning to walk in newness of life by observing all Christ commanded as we live according to the full counsel of God's Word (Matt 28:20; Rom 6:4).

Endnotes

[1] Jürgen Moltmann, *Theology of Hope; On the Ground and the Implications of a Christian Eschatology* (Minneapolis: Fortress, 1993), 22.

[2] Byung-Chul Han, *The Burnout Society* (Stanford: Stanford University Press, 2015), 18.

[3] Bruce Ellis Benson, *Graven Ideologies: Nietzsche, Derrida and Marion on Modern Idolatry* (Downers Grove: InterVarsity, 2002), 18.

[4] James Spencer, *Thinking Christian: Essays on Testimony, Accountability, and the Christian Mind* (Self-published; KSP, 2020), 18.

[5] George Orwell, *1984* (New York: Harper Collins, 1949), 3.

[6] Orwell, *1984*, 25.

[7] Orwell, *1984*, 22.

[8] Orwell, *1984*, 27.

[9] Orwell, *1984*, 169-170.

[10] Orwell, *1984*, 170.

[11] See Beale's discussion of idolatry and the manner in which we reflect what we worship in G. K. Beale, *We Become What We Worship: A Biblical Theology of Idolatry* (Downers Grove: InterVarsity, 2008).

12 Marc Lewis, "Brain Change in Addiction as Learning, Not Disease," *The New England Journal of Medicine* 379 (2018), 1551-1560

13 For a helpful summary of this concept, see Riley Clarke, "John Vervaeke on Reciprocal Narrowing," *YouTube* video, 2:51. November 12, 2021. https://youtu.be/GoBR5BPfoNo

14 In their discussion of predictive processing, Van de Cruys and Van Dessel suggest, "…the salience of prediction errors can create an increasing pressure to actively shape one's environment (or 'niche') to reduce or prevent these errors" and "As the avoidance generalizes…one's world narrows, which in turn will be mirrored in a narrowing of cognition (one's models)" (Sander Van de Cruys and Pieter Van Dessel, "Mental Distress through the Prism of Predictive Processing Theory," *Current Opinions in Psychology* 41 (2021), 110.

15 This understanding of the narrative is similar to that of Keener who notes that in the temptation narrative "the devil seeks to redefine Jesus' call; by appealing to various culturally prevalent models of power to suggest how Jesus should use his God-given power" (Craig S. Keener, *The Gospel of Matthew: A Socio-Rhetorical Commentary* [Grand Rapids: Eerdmans, 2009], 139).

16 Osborne suggests that Satan seeks "to deceive Jesus into placing self-interest above obeying his Father's will" with each temptation tests Jesus' commitment God (Grant R. Osborne, *Matthew* [Grand Rapids: Zondervan, 2010], 131).

17 Spencer, *Thinking Christian*, 131.

18 René Girard, *Deceit, Desire, and the Novel: Self and Other in Literary Structure* (Baltimore: Johns Hopkins, 1965), 12.

19 Girard, *Deceit, Desire, and the Novel*, 3.

20 Girard, *Deceit, Desire, and the Novel*, 3.

21 Bourdieu generally considers four types of capital: economic, cultural, social, and symbolic (Pierre Bourdieu, "The Forms of Capital," in *Handbook of Theory and Research for the Sociology of Education* [New York: Greenwood], 243). Economic capital consists of wealth-building assets such as money and property. Cultural, social, and symbolic capital tends to include status-building assets such as educational credentials, social connections, and networks, or marks of belonging within a given community. Regarding marks, an example might include one's knowledge of the Bible, which tends to be status-bearing regardless of educational credentialing. It might also include advocating for a particular

political position (e.g., pro-life), which signals one's virtuosity in a given community.

[22] Pierre Bourdieu, *Outline of a Theory of Practice* (Cambridge: Cambridge University Press, 1977), 77.

[23] M. A. Hogg and S. A. Reid, "Social Identity, Self-Categorization, and the Communication of Group Norms," *Communication Theory* 16 (2006), 10.

[24] Bourdieu, *Outline of a Theory of Practice*, 77.

[25] Spencer, *Thinking Christian*, 174.

[26] Johan Huizinga, "A Definition of the Concept of History," in *Philosophy and History: Essays Presented to Ernst Cassirer* ed. R. Klibansky and H. J. Paton (New York: Harper and Row, 1963), 6.

[27] The "present," if viewed on a moment-to-moment basis is difficult to grasp because it is constantly becoming the past. In this essay, "present" is considered through what sociologist Jeffrey Olick identifies as a profile, which might be akin to a snapshot in time that allows us to pause time for the purposes of evaluation and reflection. See Jeffrey K. Olick, *The Politics of Regret: On Collective Memory and Historical Responsibility* (New York: Routledge, 2007), 107-109.

[28] Charles Taylor, *Modern Social Imaginaries* (Durham: Duke University Press, 2004).

[29] Taylor, *Modern Social Imaginaries*, 83.

[30] Taylor, *Modern Social Imaginaries*, 83.

[31] "Reconstruction" does not entail fiction. In other words, when we reconstruct the past, we are not "inventing" it, but combining information in the present according to patterns made up of influential aspects of the past and present. Reconstruction involves selection as we have to determine which present information is important to us and, often in a relatively seamless process, how that information may be combined with information from the past.

[32] Carolyn Marvin and David W. Ingle, *Blood Sacrifice and the Nation: Totem Rituals and the American Flag* (Cambridge: Cambridge University Press, 199), 129.

[33] We continue to practice some of these rituals in the form of baptism and the Lord's Supper. The Old Testament Sabbath and various festivals were intended to remind

Israel of God's past and present activity among them. They reinforced a theological view of the world. Beyond more formal rituals, however, we can also practice in our daily lives as well. For further discussion on this idea, see Bruce Ellis Benson, *Liturgy as a Way of Life: Embodying the Arts in Christian Worship* (Grand Rapids: Baker, 2013).

[34] William T. Cavanaugh, *Torture and Eucharist* (Malden: Blackwell, 1998), 65. Addressing the "anti-liturgy" of torture under the Pinochet regime in Chile, Cavanaugh suggests, "Modern torture as practice in Chile is, therefore, not simply a contest over the visible, physical body; it is better understood as a contest over the social *imagination*, in which bodies are the battleground" (57). His perspective could be broadened to other "anti-liturgies" that entice us to submit to activities that involve "bodies and bodily movements in an enacted drama which both makes real the power of the state and constitutes an act of worship of that mysterious power" (30). Cavanaugh's emphasis on the state is related to his analysis of the Pinochet regime. It would seem that other sorts of power could easily be substituted into his description of "anti-liturgy."

[35] Robert W. Jenson, *Systematic Theology, vol 1: The Triune God* (New York: Oxford University Press, 1997), 63.

[36] Deryck Sheriffs, *The Friendship of the Lord: An Old Testament Spirituality* (Eugene: Wipf and Stock, 2004), 296.

[37] Spencer, *Thinking Christian*, 172.

[38] Richard Bauckham, *Who Is God?: Key Moments of Biblical Revelation* (Grand Rapids: Baker, 2020), 13.

[39] Bruce K. Waltke, *An Old Testament Theology: An Exegetical, Canonical, and Thematic Approach* (Grand Rapids: Zondervan, 2007), 162.

[40] Jay Sklar, *Leviticus: An Introduction and Commentary* (Downers Grove: InterVarsity, 2014), 155.

[41] For more on the Exodus narrative and God's unique liberation see Bryan C. Babcock, James Spencer, and Russell L. Meek, *Trajectories: A Gospel-Centered Introduction to Old Testament Theology* (Eugene: Pickwick, 2018), 67-70.

[42] Mark A. Noll, *Jesus Christ and the Life of the Mind* (Grand Rapids: Eerdmans, 2011), 152.

[43] Dwight L. Moody, *Men of the Bible* (Chicago: The Bible Institute Colportage

Association, 1898), 7.

44 Spencer, *Thinking Christian*, 25.

45 Christopher D. Bader, Joseph O. Baker, L. Edward Day, and Ann Gordon, *Fear Itself: The Causes and Consequences of Fear in America* (New York: New York University, 2020), 23.

46 Bader, *Fear Itself*, 23.

47 It seems clear that social media has similar effects though not necessarily in relation to specific fears. Note, for instance, the linkage of social media, specifically Facebook, to depression in college students in Luca Braghieri, Roee Levy, and Alexey Makarin, "Social Media and Mental Health," July 28, 2022. Available at SSRN: https://ssrn.com/abstract=3919760. The paper is forthcoming in *American Economic Review*. See also the internal Facebook documents which noted Instagram's significantly detrimental effects on young women ("Facebook's Documents about Instagram and Teens, Published," The Wall Street Journal online, September 29, 2021, https://www.wsj.com/articles/facebook-documents-instagram-teens-11632953840).

48 As I have noted elsewhere, media has always involved selection, distribution, and the determination of a point-of-view or "angle" on specific stories and topics. The difference, at this point, involves the frequency of distribution, the economic drivers of journalism, and the tactics used within the "attention economy." See Spencer, *Thinking Christian*, 77-93, 121-136. On the attention economy see Karen Nelson-Field, *The Attention Economy and How Media Works: Simple Truths for Marketers* (Springer Nature, 2020).

49 Relevance realization has become an emerging notion in cognitive psychology. The general idea is that as we interact with our environment we tend to identity more and less relevant aspects of that environment through "the selective direction of attention, the appraisal of value and the rationing and commitment of processing resources" (John Vervaeke and Leonardo Ferraro, "Relevance, Meaning and the Cognitive Science of Wisdom," in *The Scientific Study of Personal Wisdom: From Contemplative Traditions to Neuroscience* ed. Michel Ferrari and Nic M. Weststrate [New York: Springer, 2013], 31).

50 Those forsaken by God experience a sense of abandonment in which God's protective, blessing hand is removed, and the horrors of a fallen world are fully experienced. While God remains present (as his omnipresence suggests), he allows those he forsakes to experience life without him for a period of time. The focus of our attention that gives us hope and cause to endure fades away and we are left to stare out at a world

we cannot hope to control with only our own meager strength.

51 Spencer, *Thinking Christian*, 133.

52 Engel v. Vitale did not ban prayer in schools overall. Students were still allowed to pray. However, the state, as represented by the public schools, could not hold prayers of any sort (Christian or otherwise) even if students could opt-out of the prayers.

53 John Kennedy, "Pray at Home, Kennedy Answer to Supreme Court Ruling," *YouTube*, 1:24, April 27, 2022. https://youtu.be/_7TA1th-rEc.

54 See also School District of Abington Township, Pennsylvania v. Schempp from 1963, which prohibited school-sponsored devotional readings form the Bible and the recitation of the Lord's prayer.

55 Engel v. Vitale only banned school-sponsored prayer based on the Supreme Court's interpretation of the Establishment Clause. However, students and teachers would have been free to pray together in public schools so long as that activity was not school sponsored. The recent finding in Kennedy v. Bremerton School District affirms, "The Free Exercise and Free Speech Clauses of the First Amendment protect an individual engaging in a personal religious observance from governmental reprisal; the Constitution neither mandates nor permits the government to suppress such religious expression" (Kennedy v. Bremerton School District, 991 U.S. 1 [2022]). I am not making a historical assertion here. The socio-cultural matrix in the 1960's may well have precluded individual and corporate prayer even if such prayer was not school sponsored. In principle, however, the court's decision in Engel v. Vitale did not preclude the practice of prayer as such. See the syllabus for the decision at https://www.supremecourt.gov/opinions/21pdf/21-418_i425.pdf.

56 By the time the First Amendment was ratified in 1791, there were already established churches in some states, which led to a variety of problems between established and non-established Christian churches. Note the citations below from Isaac Backus for an introduction to some of these issues. In addition to established churches, some states included religious tests for civil service that were explicitly Christian in nature requiring, for instance, the explicit profession of belief "in God the Father, and in Jesus Christ His only Son, and in the Holy Ghost…" (See Article 6, Clause 3 of the Delaware Constitution of 1776, Art. 22 at https://press-pubs.uchicago.edu/founders/documents/a6_3s2.html/). Concerns of the Philadelphia Synagogue in the early 1780's related to the inclusion of Christian religious tests for civil service facilitated a changed to the Pennsylvania state constitution in 1790 (*Proceedings Relative to the Calling of the Conventions of 1776 and 1790*, 216-18, 376). By removing the

explicitly Christian language from the religious test, Pennsylvania allowed for a broader religious and moral sensibility without requiring specifically Christian professions. We see a similar religious, though not Christian, interest represented in the Virginia Statute for Religious Freedom. Based on a majority vote to remove language about Jesus Christ, Thomas Jefferson infers that the state sought to provide religious freedom to "the Jew, the Gentile, the Christian, the Mahometan, the Hindoo, and infidel of every denomination" (Thomas Jefferson, "Autobiography Draft Fragment," January 6 through July 27. -07-27, 1821. Manuscript/Mixed Material. http://www.loc.gov/item/mtjbib024000/). These relatively early examples of tension related to non-Christian religious freedom do not negate early Christian influence in the United States. However, they do seem to suggest that Christian adherence and representation were not essential to national identity as often seems to be suggested in the phrase "Christian nation."

[57] Writing in 1778, Baptist pastor Isaac Backus asserts, "it is impossible to blend church and state together, without violating our Lord's commands to both" (Isaac Backus, "Policy, as well as Honesty, Forbids the Use of Secular Force in Religious Affairs," 1778. Early English Books Online Text Creation Partnership, 2011, http://name.umdl.umich.edu/N12813.001.001, accessed 25 October 2022). Backus was an early advocate against government establishment of various sorts that would privilege one denomination over another. His argues, "the teaching the fear of God by the precepts of men" would bring "confusion and ruin" and that "rulers, ministers and people, ought to improve all their influence, in their several stations, to promote and support true religion by gospel means and methods" (Isaac Backus, "Government and Liberty Described; And Ecclesiastical Tyranny Exposed," 1778. Early English Books Online Text Creation Partnership, 2011, http://name.umdl.umich.edu/N12452.001.001, accessed 25 October 2022).

[58] Michael Suk-Young Chwe, *Rational Ritual: Culture, Coordination, and Common Knowledge* (Princeton: Princeton University Press, 2001), 3.

[59] In the 2022 State of Theology report, 35% of respondents "strongly agree" and 32% "somewhat agree" with the statement: "Worshiping alone or with one's family is a valid replacement for regularly attending church." See "The State of Theology" at https://thestateoftheology.com.

[60] Michael Cartwright, John Berkman, and Stanley Hauerwas, *The Hauerwas Reader*, (Durham: Duke University Press, 2001), 526.

[61] Lifeway research notes that 44% of pastors identified "people's political views" as one of the top five "people dynamics at church" that are "challenging to pastors." See "Apathy in Churches Looms Large for Pastors," Lifeway Research online,

May 10, 2022, https://research.lifeway.com/2022/05/10/apathy-in-churches-looms-large-for-pastors/.

62 Spencer, *Thinking Christian*, 134.

63 For the original quote "Breakfast in Washington," *Time* 63, no 7, February 1954, 49.

64 Robert Jeffress, "America is a Christian Nation," *YouTube*, 15:45, July 3, 2022. https://youtu.be/lcpADZ2zn4w.

65 Even the Ten Commandments, which are often referred to as a basic moral code of sorts, begin with deeply theological statements that require unwavering loyalty to the Lord. As such moral and ethical behavior can, at best, function in a way similar to Israelite law which governs behavior but cannot transform the heart or cultivate devotion. See Averbeck's discussion of the Law's weakness in Richard E. Averbeck, *The Old Testament Law for the Life of the Church: Reading the Torah in the Light of Christ*, (Downers Grove: InterVarsity, 2022), 283-309.

66 Jeffress makes clear that salvation comes through an individual's acceptance of Jesus Christ. As such, it might seem plausible to assume that he is not assuming mass conversion as a pre-condition for the United States to be "a nations whose God is the Lord." Given his quotation of Warren, it would appear that Jeffress has in mind a more generic return to something approximating the Judeo-Christian ethic or the "Christian heritage" of the United States in which "Christianity was elevated above every other 'imposter religion,' to use the terminology of the Supreme Court in 1892" (Robert Jeffress, *Outrageous Truth: Seven Absolutes You Can Still Believe* [Colorado Springs: Waterbrook, 2008, 189). While Jeffress connects the ideas of diversity and pluralism to idolatry in his book, he doesn't deal with the conceptual and, I would argue, the theological gaps, between his application of, for instance Psalm 33:12 ("Blessed is the nation whose God is the Lord"), which refers to Israel and not to the nations more generally as is suggested by the parallel line in Psalm 33:12 ("…the people whom he has chosen as his heritage) left uncited by Jeffress. As such, Jeffress seems to be advocating for some abstracted notion of morality which would not require mass conversion.

67 Neither is Paul seeking to eliminate Jewish and Gentile identity. He is more interested in ensuring that the "in-Christ" identity of Jews and Gentiles to govern the Jewish and Gentile identities of individuals who accept Christ. For a more in-depth treatment of these matters see J. Brian Tucker, *You Belong to Christ: Paul and the Formation of Social Identity in 1 Corinthians 1-4* (Eugene: Pickwick, 2010).

[68] It seems to me that the United States is a "Christian nation" in this latter sense. There is little evidence to deny some limited influence of Christianity at the nation's founding though Christians and Christian principles were not properly "governing" in the sense that we might ascribe to the reformation doctrine of *sola scriptura*. The influence is evident, but not primary allowing for drift away from Christianity and the ethics extrapolated from it.

[69] Jeffress is not alone in his understanding. In a 2022 survey from the Trafalgar Group and the Convention of States Action, 52.6% of Americans surveyed said that "the moral lessons found in the holidays of Easter and Passover" were "very important" "to ensuring a strong America for future generations." An additional 20% said that those moral lessons were somewhat important. Given the lack of clarity regarding just what those "moral lessons" might be when separated from the crucifixion and resurrection of Christ, it would seem that many Americans are making a connection between being sufficiently moral and maintaining national strength. See "Nationwide Issues Survey," April 2022. https://www.thetrafalgargroup.org/wp-content/uploads/2022/04/COSA-EasterLessons-Full-Report-0410.pdf.

[70] Spencer, *Thinking Christian*, 72.

[71] Daniel Kahneman, *Thinking, Fast and Slow* (New York: Farrar, 2011), 13.

[72] Kahneman, *Thinking, Fast and Slow*, 13.

[73] Kahneman, *Thinking, Fast and Slow*, 20. There is some debate within the decision-making science literature regarding the importance and value of intuition in decision-making. Klein, for instance, views intuitive, fast judgments in a more positive light than Kahneman suggesting, "I believe it is important to counterbalance the negative impression of System 1 with a sense of awe and appreciation about the insights we create and the discoveries we make…the process of gaining insights…balances the worries about decision biases" (Gary Klein, *Seeing What Others Don't: The Remarkable Ways We Gain Insights* [New York: Public Affairs, 2013], 98). Klein's framework is helpful in highlighting the necessity of mental flexibility expressed in a willingness to question our intuition when confronted with information that does not fit our current pattern so that intuition can turn into insight.

[74] Kahneman, *Thinking, Fast and Slow*, 85.

[75] Kahneman, *Thinking, Fast and Slow*, 20.

[76] Kevin J. Vanhoozer, *Hearers and Doers: A Pastor's Guide to Making Disciples through Scripture and Doctrine* (Bellingham: Lexham, 2019), 7-8.

77 Lennart Boström, "Retribution and Wisdom Literature," in *Interpreting Old Testament Wisdom Literature* ed. David G. Firth and Lindsay Wilson (Downers Grove: InterVarsity, 2017), 135. Notice that the rigid application of the retribution principle tends to subject not only Job to its logic, but God. The friends cannot fathom a world in which God is not in some way governed by the retribution principle in so much as this particular construal of justice becomes essential to justice as such and, so, becomes essential to God.

78 Elaine A. Phillips, "Speaking Truthfully: Job's Friends and Job," *Bulletin for Biblical Research* 18 (2008), 35.

79 Francis I. Anderson, *Job* (Downers Grove: InterVarsity, 2008), 105.

80 Anderson, *Job*, 104.

81 Samuel Well, *Improvisation: The Drama of Christian Ethics* (Grand Rapids: Brazos, 2004), 75.

82 Klein suggests that insight is derived through a variety of "paths" in which one's current paradigms are challenged, shifted, or otherwise modified by new information. For a graphic summary see Klein, *Seeing What Others Don't*, 105.

83 Spencer, *Thinking Christian*, 56.

84 James Clear, *Atomic Habits: An Easy and Proven Way to Build Good Habits and Break Bad Ones* (New York: Penguin, 2018), 46.

85 Nick Bostrom, "The Vulnerable World Hypothesis," *Global Policy* 10 (2019), 457.

86 Bostrom, "The Vulnerable World Hypothesis," 457-458.

87 Bostrom, "The Vulnerable World Hypothesis," 458.

88 For a review of some such trends see Ronald Baily and Marian L. Tupy, *Ten Global Trends Every Smart Person Should Know: And Many Others You Will Find Interesting* (Washington, D. C.: Cato Institute, 2020).

89 Critiquing, though not *condemning*, the formation of nation states, political scientist James Scott argues, "certain kinds of states, driven by utopian plans and an authoritarian disregard for the values, desires, and objections of their subjects, are indeed a mortal threat to human well-being" (James C. Scott, *Seeing Like a State: How Certain Schemes to Improve the Human Condition Have Failed* [New Haven: Yale University Press, 1998], 7).

Not condemning the state is important. Scott is not arguing for a future without some form of state authority but that the convergence of certain state features become problematic for human flourishing. For a discussion of these features see Scott, *Seeing Like a State*, 3-5. He goes on to suggest that we are "left to weigh judiciously the benefits of certain state interventions against their costs" (Scott, *Seeing Like a State*, 7).

[90] For an application of this sort of logic, see James Spencer, "Let Us Build a Metaverse," TownHall, April 12, 2022, https://townhall.com/columnists/jamesspencer/2022/04/12/let-us-build-a-metaverse-n2605762. See also the discussion of "revenge effects" caused when "new structures, devices, and organisms react with real people in real situations in ways we could not foresee" (Edward Tenner, *Why Things Bite Back: Technology and the Revenge of Unintended Consequences* [New York: Random House, 1997], 11).

[91] Friedrich Nietzsche, *Twilight of the Idols* (Oxford: Oxford University Press, 1998), 41.

[92] Dallas Willard, *The Spirit of the Disciplines: Understanding How God Changes Lives* (New York: Harper Collins, 1988), 10.

[93] Donald P. McNeill, Douglas A. Morrison, and Henri J. M. Nouwen, *Compassion: A Reflection on the Christian Life* (New York: Doubleday, 1982), 88.

[94] McNeil, Morrison, and Nouwen, *Compassion*, 88.

[95] Spencer, *Thinking Christian*, 4.

[96] Alexander Solzhenitsyn, "Live Not by Lies," The Aleksandr Solzhenitsyn Center, 1974, accessed October 25, 2022, https://www.solzhenitsyncenter.org/live-not-by-lies.

[97] Solzhenitsyn, "Live Not by Lies."

[98] Solzhenitsyn, "Live Not by Lies."

[99] Solzhenitsyn, "Live Not by Lies."

[100] Solzhenitsyn, "Live Not by Lies."

[101] Solzhenitsyn, "Live Not by Lies."

[102] Solzhenitsyn, "Live Not by Lies."

[103] C. A. J. Coady, *Testimony: A Philosophical Study* (Oxford: Clarendon, 1992), 52.

[104] John Vervaeke, Christopher Mastropietro, and Filip Miscevic, *Zombies in Western Culture: A Twenty-First Century Crisis* (Cambridge: Open Book, 2017), 86. They go on to note, "We can build a commitment to models of thinking and acting solely based on their salience. We can condition ourselves into retaining an idea regardless of its integrity (Vervaeke, Mastropietro, and Miscevic, *Zombies in Western Culture*, 87).

[105] Philip F. Esler, "Group Norms and Prototypes in Matthew 5:3-12: A Social Identity Interpretation of the Matthaean Beatitudes," in *T & T Clark Handbook to Social Identity in the New Testament* ed. J. Brian Tucker and Coleman A. Baker (London: Bloomsbury, 2016), 169.

[106] Dietrich Bonhoeffer, *Ethics*, trans. Reinhard Krauss, Charles C. West, and Douglas W. Stott (Minneapolis: Fortress, 2005), 231.

[107] Vervaeke, Mastropietro, and Miscevic, *Zombies in Western Culture*, 86.

[108] Spencer, *Thinking Christian*, 100.

[109] Moises Naim, *The End of Power: From Boardrooms to Battlefields and Churches to States, Why Being in Charge Isn't What It Used to Be* (New York: Basic, 2013), 229.

[110] Kevin J. Vanhoozer and Owen Strachan, *The Pastor as Public Theologian: Reclaiming a Lost Vision* (Grand Rapids: Baker, 2015), 17.

[111] Spencer, *Thinking Christian*, 65.

[112] Spencer, *Thinking Christian*, 93.

[113] Slavoj Žižek, "Maybe We Just Need a Different Chicken… Politeness and Civility in the Function of Contemporary Ideology," *YouTube* video, 9:58, September 15, 2008. https://youtu.be/OtByLzG5PsE.

[114] Žižek addresses this incompleteness elsewhere noting, "The very concept of ideology implies a kind of basic, constitutive naïveté: the misrecognition of its own presuppositions, of its own effective condition, a distance, a divergence between so-called social reality and our distorted representation, our false consciousness of it" (Slavoj Žižek, *The Sublime Object of Ideology* [London: Verso, 1989], 28). He goes on to argue that we tend to develop ways "to blind ourselves to the structuring power of ideological fantasy" so that

"even if we do not take things seriously, even if we keep an ironical distance, we are still doing them" (Žižek, *The Sublime Object of Ideology*, 33). The point is that ideology does not fit squarely in our minds as cognitive constructions. As such, "The fundamental level of ideology…is not of an illusion masking the real state of things but that of an (unconscious) fantasy structuring our social reality itself (Žižek, *The Sublime Object of Ideology*, 33). Ideology is, on some level, the assertion (conscious or unconscious) that our incomplete maps are complete.

[115] Michael Freeden, *Ideology: A Very Short Introduction* (Oxford: Oxford University Press, 2003), 3.

[116] James J. Gibson, *The Ecological Approach to Visual Perception* (Hillsdale: Lawrence Erlbaum Associates, 1986), 139.

[117] While Monmonier doesn't necessarily have ideology in mind, the analogy between ideologies and physical/digital maps seems appropriate. See Mark Monmonier, *How to Lie with Maps* (Chicago: University of Chicago Press, 2018), 1.

[118] Christ certainly addressed more "institutional" issues with regard to the Pharisees and the Jewish religious community (Matt 21:12-17; 23:1-36); however, he seldom addresses Rome (Matt 22:15-22). Rather than push for institutional reform, Jesus encourages his follows to live with distinction (Matt 5:1-12) and to showcase God's wisdom as the "salt of the earth" and "light of the world" (Matt 5:13-16). The apostles seem to have adopted a similar approach (1 Cor7:17-24). That does not mean we should not address the politics of the day; however, it is worth noting that political activity cannot be the end of our work anymore than, for example, writing a book can be. Our positions should not keep us from both loving God and loving neighbor with neighbor being understood in terms of the parable of the Good Samaritan (Lk 10:25-37). Our neighbors are not simply those who agree with our positions, but those who disagree with them.

[119] Spencer, *Thinking Christian*, 102.

[120] George Will, *The Pursuit of Happiness and Other Sobering Thoughts* (New York: Harper and Row, 1978), 3.

Made in the USA
Coppell, TX
08 February 2023